T0248441

On
Performance
Management

HBR's 10 Must Reads series is the definitive collection of ideas and best practices for aspiring and experienced leaders alike. These books offer essential reading selected from the pages of *Harvard Business Review* on topics critical to the success of every manager.

Titles include:

HBR's 10 Must Reads 2015
HBR's 10 Must Reads 2016
HBR's 10 Must Reads 2017
HBR's 10 Must Reads 2018
HBR's 10 Must Reads 2019
HBR's 10 Must Reads 2020
HBR's 10 Must Reads 2021
HBR's 10 Must Reads 2022
HBR's 10 Must Reads 2023
HBR's 10 Must Reads for CEOs
HBR's 10 Must Reads for New Managers
HBR's 10 Must Reads on AI, Analytics, and the New Machine Age
HBR's 10 Must Reads on Boards
HBR's 10 Must Reads on Building a Great Culture
HBR's 10 Must Reads on Business Model Innovation
HBR's 10 Must Reads on Career Resilience
HBR's 10 Must Reads on Change Management (Volumes 1 and 2)
HBR's 10 Must Reads on Collaboration
HBR's 10 Must Reads on Communication (Volumes 1 and 2)
HBR's 10 Must Reads on Creativity
HBR's 10 Must Reads on Design Thinking
HBR's 10 Must Reads on Diversity
HBR's 10 Must Reads on Emotional Intelligence
HBR's 10 Must Reads on Entrepreneurship and Startups
HBR's 10 Must Reads on High Performance
HBR's 10 Must Reads on Innovation
HBR's 10 Must Reads on Leadership (Volumes 1 and 2)

HBR'S 10 MUST READS

On
Performance
Management

HARVARD BUSINESS REVIEW PRESS
Boston, Massachusetts

Copyright 2023 Harvard Business School Publishing Corporation

The web addresses referenced in this book were live and correct at the time of the book's publication but may be subject to change.

Cataloging-in-Publication data is forthcoming.

ISBN: 978-1-64782-521-8
eISBN: 978-1-64782-522-5

The paper used in this publication meets the requirements of the American National Standard for Permanence of Paper for Publications and Documents in Libraries and Archives Z39.48-1992.

Contents

On
**Performance
Management**

The Performance Management Revolution

by Peter Cappelli and Anna Tavis

WHEN BRIAN JENSEN TOLD HIS AUDIENCE of HR executives that Colorcon wasn't bothering with annual reviews anymore, they were appalled. This was in 2002, during his tenure as the drugmaker's head of global human resources. In his presentation at the Wharton School, Jensen explained that Colorcon had found a more effective way of reinforcing desired behaviors and managing performance: Supervisors were giving people instant feedback, tying it to individuals' own goals, and handing out small weekly bonuses to employees they saw doing good things.

Back then the idea of abandoning the traditional appraisal process—and all that followed from it—seemed heretical. But now, by some estimates, more than one-third of U.S. companies are doing just that. From Silicon Valley to New York, and in offices across the world, firms are replacing annual reviews with frequent, informal check-ins between managers and employees.

As you might expect, technology companies such as Adobe, Juniper Systems, Dell, Microsoft, and IBM have led the way. Yet they've been joined by a number of professional services firms (Deloitte, Accenture, PwC), early adopters in other industries (Gap, Lear, OppenheimerFunds), and even General Electric, the longtime role model for traditional appraisals.

Without question, rethinking performance management is at the top of many executive teams' agendas, but what drove the change in this direction? Many factors. In a recent article for *People + Strategy,* a Deloitte manager referred to the review process as "an investment of 1.8 million hours across the firm that didn't fit our business needs anymore." One *Washington Post* business writer called it a "rite of corporate kabuki" that restricts creativity, generates mountains of paperwork, and serves no real purpose. Others have described annual reviews as a last-century practice and blamed them for a lack of collaboration and innovation. Employers are also finally acknowledging that both supervisors and subordinates despise the appraisal process—a perennial problem that feels more urgent now that the labor market is picking up and concerns about retention have returned.

But the biggest limitation of annual reviews—and, we have observed, the main reason more and more companies are dropping them—is this: With their heavy emphasis on financial rewards and punishments and their end-of-year structure, they hold people accountable for past behavior at the expense of improving current performance and grooming talent for the future, both of which are critical for organizations' long-term survival. In contrast, regular conversations about performance and development change the focus to building the workforce your organization needs to be competitive both today and years from now. Business researcher Josh Bersin estimates that about 70% of multinational companies are moving toward this model, even if they haven't arrived quite yet.

The tension between the traditional and newer approaches stems from a long-running dispute about managing people: Do you "get what you get" when you hire your employees? Should you focus mainly on motivating the strong ones with money and getting rid of the weak ones? Or are employees malleable? Can you change the way they perform through effective coaching and management and intrinsic rewards such as personal growth and a sense of progress on the job?

With traditional appraisals, the pendulum had swung too far toward the former, more transactional view of performance, which became hard to support in an era of low inflation and tiny merit-pay budgets. Those who still hold that view are railing against the recent emphasis on improvement and growth over accountability. But the

Idea in Brief

The Problem

By emphasizing individual accountability for past results, traditional appraisals give short shrift to improving current performance and developing talent for the future. That can hinder long-term competitiveness.

The Solution

To better support employee development, many organizations are dropping or radically changing their annual review systems in favor of giving people less formal, more frequent feedback that follows the natural cycle of work.

The Outlook

This shift isn't just a fad—real business needs are driving it. Support at the top is critical, though. Some firms that have struggled to go entirely without ratings are trying a "third way": assigning multiple ratings several times a year to encourage employees' growth.

new perspective is unlikely to be a flash in the pan because, as we will discuss, it is being driven by business needs, not imposed by HR.

First, though, let's consider how we got to this point—and how companies are faring with new approaches.

How We Got Here

Historical and economic context has played a large role in the evolution of performance management over the decades. When human capital was plentiful, the focus was on which people to let go, which to keep, and which to reward—and for those purposes, traditional appraisals (with their emphasis on individual accountability) worked pretty well. But when talent was in shorter supply, as it is now, developing people became a greater concern—and organizations had to find new ways of meeting that need.

From accountability to development

Appraisals can be traced back to the U.S. military's "merit rating" system, created during World War I to identify poor performers for discharge or transfer. After World War II, about 60% of U.S. companies were using them (by the 1960s, it was closer to 90%). Though seniority rules determined pay increases and promotions for unionized work-ers, strong merit scores meant good advancement prospects for man-agers. At least initially, *improving* performance was an afterthought.

And then a severe shortage of managerial talent caused a shift in organizational priorities: Companies began using appraisals to develop employees into supervisors, and especially managers into executives. In a famous 1957 HBR article, social psychologist Doug-las McGregor argued that subordinates should, with feedback from the boss, help set their performance goals and assess themselves—a process that would build on their strengths and potential. This "Theory Y" approach to management—he coined the term later on—assumed that employees wanted to perform well and would do so if supported properly. ("Theory X" assumed you had to motivate people with material rewards and punishments.) McGregor noted one drawback to the approach he advocated: Doing it right would take managers several days per subordinate each year.

By the early 1960s, organizations had become so focused on developing future talent that many observers thought that track-ing past performance had fallen by the wayside. Part of the problem was that supervisors were reluctant to distinguish good performers from bad. One study, for example, found that 98% of federal govern-ment employees received "satisfactory" ratings, while only 2% got either of the other two outcomes: "unsatisfactory" or "outstanding." After running a well-publicized experiment in 1964, General Electric concluded it was best to split the appraisal process into separate dis-cussions about accountability and development, given the conflicts between them. Other companies followed suit.

Back to accountability

In the 1970s, however, a shift began. Inflation rates shot up, and merit-based pay took center stage in the appraisal process. During that period, annual wage increases really mattered. Supervisors often had discretion to give raises of 20% or more to strong performers, to distinguish them from the sea of employees receiving basic cost-of-living raises, and getting no increase represented a substantial pay cut. With the stakes so high—and with antidiscrimination laws so recently on the books—the pressure was on to award pay more objectively. As a result, accountability became a higher priority than development for many organizations.

Three other changes in the zeitgeist reinforced that shift:

First, Jack Welch became CEO of General Electric in 1981. To deal with the long-standing concern that supervisors failed to label real differences in performance, Welch championed the forced-ranking system—another military creation. Though the U.S. Army had devised it, just before entering World War II, to quickly identify a large number of officer candidates for the country's imminent military expansion, GE used it to shed people at the bottom. Equating performance with individuals' inherent capabilities (and largely ignoring their potential to grow), Welch divided his workforce into "A" players, who must be rewarded; "B" players, who should be accommodated; and "C" players, who should be dismissed. In that system, development was reserved for the "A" players—the high-potentials chosen to advance into senior positions.

Second, 1993 legislation limited the tax deductibility of executive salaries to $1 million but exempted performance-based pay. That led to a rise in outcome-based bonuses for corporate leaders—a change that trickled down to frontline managers and even hourly employees—and organizations relied even more on the appraisal process to assess merit.

Third, McKinsey's War for Talent research project in the late 1990s suggested that some employees were fundamentally more talented than others (you knew them when you saw them, the thinking went). Because such individuals were, by definition, in short supply, organizations felt they needed to take great care in tracking and rewarding them. Nothing in the McKinsey studies showed that fixed personality traits actually made certain people perform better, but that was the assumption.

So, by the early 2000s, organizations were using performance appraisals mainly to hold employees accountable and to allocate rewards. By some estimates, as many as one-third of U.S. corporations—and 60% of the *Fortune* 500—had adopted a forced-ranking system. At the same time, other changes in corporate life made it harder for the appraisal process to advance the time-consuming goals of improving individual performance and developing skills for future roles. Organizations got much flatter, which dramatically increased the number of subordinates that supervisors had to manage. The new norm was 15 to 25 direct reports (up from six before the 1960s). While overseeing more employees, supervisors were also expected to be individual contributors. So taking days to manage the performance issues of each employee, as Douglas McGregor had advocated, was impossible. Meanwhile, greater interest in lateral hiring reduced the need for internal development. Up to two-thirds of corporate jobs were filled from outside, compared with about 10% a generation earlier.

Back to development . . . again

Another major turning point came in 2005: A few years after Jack Welch left GE, the company quietly backed away from forced ranking because it fostered internal competition and undermined collaboration. Welch still defends the practice, but what he really supports is the general principle of letting people know how they are doing: "As a manager, you owe candor to your people," he wrote in the *Wall Street Journal* in 2013. "They must not be guessing about what the organization thinks of them." It's hard to argue against candor, of course. But more and more firms began questioning how useful it was to compare people with one another or even to rate them on a scale.

So the emphasis on accountability for past performance started to fade. That continued as jobs became more complex and rapidly changed shape—in that climate, it was difficult to set annual goals that would still be meaningful 12 months later. Plus, the move toward team-based work often conflicted with individual appraisals and rewards. And low inflation and small budgets for wage increases made appraisal-driven merit pay seem futile. What was the point of trying to draw performance distinctions when rewards were so trivial?

The whole appraisal process was loathed by employees anyway. Social science research showed that they hated numerical scores—they would rather be told they were "average" than given a 3 on a 5-point scale. They especially detested forced ranking. As Wharton's

Iwan Barankay demonstrated in a field setting, performance actually declined when people were rated relative to others. Nor did the ratings seem accurate. As the accumulating research on appraisal scores showed, they had as much to do with who the rater was (people gave higher ratings to those who were like them) as they did with performance.

And managers hated *doing* reviews, as survey after survey made clear. Willis Towers Watson found that 45% did not see value in the systems they used. Deloitte reported that 58% of HR executives considered reviews an ineffective use of supervisors' time. In a study by the advisory service CEB, the average manager reported spending about 210 hours—close to five weeks—doing appraisals each year.

As dissatisfaction with the traditional process mounted, high-tech firms ushered in a new way of thinking about performance. The "Agile Manifesto," created by software developers in 2001, outlined several key values—favoring, for instance, "responding to change over following a plan." It emphasized principles such as collaboration, self-organization, self-direction, and regular reflection on how to work more effectively, with the aim of prototyping more quickly and responding in real time to customer feedback and changes in requirements. Although not directed at performance per se, these principles changed the definition of effectiveness on the job—and they were at odds with the usual practice of cascading goals from the top down and assessing people against them once a year.

So it makes sense that the first significant departure from traditional reviews happened at Adobe, in 2011. The company was already using the agile method, breaking down projects into "sprints" that were immediately followed by debriefing sessions. Adobe explicitly brought this notion of constant assessment and feedback into performance management, with frequent check-ins replacing annual appraisals. Juniper Systems, Dell, and Microsoft were prominent followers.

CEB estimated in 2014 that 12% of U.S. companies had dropped annual reviews altogether. Willis Towers Watson put the figure at 8% but added that 29% were considering eliminating them or planning to do so. Deloitte reported in 2015 that only 12% of the U.S. companies it surveyed were *not* planning to rethink their performance management systems. This trend seems to be extending beyond the United States as well. PwC reports that two-thirds of large companies in the UK, for example, are in the process of changing their systems.

Three Business Reasons to Drop Appraisals

In light of that history, we see three clear business imperatives that are leading companies to abandon performance appraisals:

The return of people development

Companies are under competitive pressure to upgrade their talent management efforts. This is especially true at consulting and other professional services firms, where knowledge work is the offering—and where inexperienced college grads are turned into skilled advisers through structured training. Such firms are doubling down on development, often by putting their employees (who are deeply motivated by the potential for learning and advancement) in charge of their own growth. This approach requires rich feedback from supervisors—a need that's better met by frequent, informal check-ins than by annual reviews.

Now that the labor market has tightened and keeping good people is once again critical, such companies have been trying to eliminate "dissatisfiers" that drive employees away. Naturally, annual reviews are on that list, since the process is so widely reviled and the focus on numerical ratings interferes with the learning that people want and need to do. Replacing this system with feedback that's delivered right after client engagements helps managers do a better job of coaching and allows subordinates to process and apply the advice more effectively.

Kelly Services was the first big professional services firm to drop appraisals, in 2011. PwC tried it with a pilot group in 2013 and then discontinued annual reviews for all 200,000-plus employees. Deloitte followed in 2015, and Accenture and KPMG made similar announcements shortly thereafter. Given the sheer size of these firms, and the fact that they offer management advice to thousands of organizations, their choices are having an enormous impact on other companies. Firms that scrap appraisals are also rethinking employee management much more broadly. Accenture CEO Pierre Nanterme estimates that his firm is changing about 90% of its talent practices.

The need for agility

When rapid innovation is a source of competitive advantage, as it is now in many companies and industries, that means future needs are continually changing. Because organizations won't necessarily want employees to keep doing the same things, it doesn't make sense to hang on to a system that's built mainly to assess and hold people accountable for past or current practices. As Susan Peters, GE's head of human resources, has pointed out, businesses no longer have clear annual cycles. Projects are short-term and tend to change along the way, so employees' goals and tasks can't be plotted out a year in advance with much accuracy.

At GE a new business strategy based on innovation was the biggest reason the company recently began eliminating individual ratings and annual reviews. Its new approach to performance management is aligned with its FastWorks platform for creating products and bringing them to market, which borrows a lot from agile techniques. Supervisors still have an end-of-year summary discussion with subordinates, but the goal is to push frequent conversations with employees (GE calls them "touchpoints") and keep revisiting two basic questions: What am I doing that I should keep doing? And what am I doing that I should change? Annual goals have been replaced with shorter-term "priorities." As with many of the companies we see, GE first launched a pilot, with about 87,000 employees in 2015, before adopting the changes across the company.

The centrality of teamwork

Moving away from forced ranking and from appraisals' focus on individual accountability makes it easier to foster teamwork. This has become especially clear at retail companies like Sears and Gap—perhaps the most surprising early innovators in appraisals. Sophisticated customer service now requires frontline and back-office employees to work together to keep shelves stocked and manage customer flow, and traditional systems don't enhance performance at the team level or help track collaboration.

Gap supervisors still give workers end-of-year assessments, but only to summarize performance discussions that happen throughout the year and to set pay increases accordingly. Employees still have goals, but as at other companies, the goals are short-term (in this case, quarterly). Now two years into its new system, Gap reports far more satisfaction with its performance process and the best-ever completion of store-level goals. Nonetheless, Rob Ollander-Krane, Gap's senior director of organization performance effectiveness, says the company needs further improvement in setting stretch goals and focusing on team performance.

Implications

All three reasons for dropping annual appraisals argue for a system that more closely follows the natural cycle of work. Ideally, conversations between managers and employees occur when projects finish, milestones are reached, challenges pop up, and so forth—allowing people to solve problems in current performance while also developing skills for the future. At most companies, managers take the lead in setting near-term goals, and employees drive career conversations throughout the year. In the words of one Deloitte manager: "The conversations are more holistic. They're about goals and strengths, not just about past performance."

Perhaps most important, companies are overhauling performance management because their businesses require the change. That's true whether they're professional services firms that must develop people in order to compete, companies that need to deliver ongoing performance feedback to support rapid innovation, or retailers that need better coordination between the sales floor and the back office to serve their customers.

Of course, many HR managers worry: If we can't get supervisors to have good conversations with subordinates once a year, how can we expect them to do so more frequently, without the support of the usual appraisal process? It's a valid question—but we see reasons to be optimistic.

As GE found in 1964 and as research has documented since, it is extraordinarily difficult to have a serious, open discussion about problems while also dishing out consequences such as low merit pay. The end-of-year review was also an excuse for delaying feedback until then, at which point both the supervisor and the employee were likely to have forgotten what had happened months earlier. Both of those constraints disappear when you take away the annual review. Additionally, almost all companies that have dropped traditional appraisals have invested in training supervisors to talk more about development with their employees—and they are checking with subordinates to make sure that's happening.

Moving to an informal system requires a culture that will keep the continuous feedback going. As Megan Taylor, Adobe's director of business partnering, pointed out at a recent conference, it's difficult to sustain that if it's not happening organically. Adobe, which has gone totally numberless but still gives merit increases based on informal assessments, reports that regular conversations between managers and their employees are now occurring without HR's prompting. Deloitte, too, has found that its new model of frequent, informal check-ins has led to more meaningful discussions, deeper insights, and greater employee satisfaction. (For more details, see "Reinventing Performance Management," HBR, April 2015.) The firm started to go numberless like Adobe but then switched to assigning employees several numbers four times a year, to give them rolling feedback on different dimensions. Jeffrey Orlando, who heads up development and performance at Deloitte, says the company has been tracking the effects on business results, and they've been positive so far.

Challenges That Persist

The greatest resistance to abandoning appraisals, which is something of a revolution in human resources, comes from HR itself. The reason is simple: Many of the processes and systems that HR has built over the years revolve around those performance ratings. Experts in employment law had advised organizations to standardize practices, develop objective criteria to justify every employment decision, and

A talent management time line

The tug-of-war between accountability and development over the decades

WWI	WWII	1940s	1950s	1960s	1970s
The U.S. military created a merit-rating system to flag and dismiss poor performers.	The army devised forced ranking to identify enlisted soldiers with the potential to become officers.	About 60% of U.S. companies were using appraisals to document workers' performance and allocate rewards.	Social psychologist Douglas McGregor argued for engaging employees in assessments and goal setting.	Led by General Electric, companies began splitting appraisals into separate discussions about accountability and growth to give development its due.	Inflation rates shot up, and organizations felt pressure to award merit pay more objectively, so accountability again became the priority in the appraisal process.

1980s

Jack Welch championed forced ranking at GE to reward top performers, accommodate those in the middle, and get rid of those at the bottom.

1990s

McKinsey's War for Talent study pointed to a shortage of capable executives and reinforced the emphasis on assessing and rewarding performance.

2000

Organizations got flatter, which dramatically increased the number of direct reports each manager had, making it harder to invest time in developing them.

2011

Kelly Services was the first big professional services firm to drop appraisals, and other major firms followed suit, emphasizing frequent, informal feedback.

Adobe ended annual performance reviews, in keeping with the famous "Agile Manifesto" and the notion that annual targets were irrelevant to the way its business operated.

2016

Deloitte, PwC, and others that tried going numberless are reinstating performance ratings but using more than one number and keeping the new emphasis on developmental feedback.

☐ Accountability focus
⁙ Development focus
☐ A hybrid "third way"

document all relevant facts. Taking away appraisals flies in the face of that advice—and it doesn't necessarily solve every problem that they failed to address.

Here are some of the challenges that organizations still grapple with when they replace the old performance model with new approaches:

Aligning individual and company goals

In the traditional model, business objectives and strategies cascaded down the organization. All the units, and then all the individual employees, were supposed to establish their goals to reflect and reinforce the direction set at the top. But this approach works only when business goals are easy to articulate and held constant over the course of a year. As we've discussed, that's often not the case these days, and employee goals may be pegged to specific projects. So as projects unfold and tasks change, how do you coordinate individual priorities with the goals for the whole enterprise, especially when the business objectives are short-term and must rapidly adapt to market shifts? It's a new kind of problem to solve, and the jury is still out on how to respond.

Rewarding performance

Appraisals gave managers a clear-cut way of tying rewards to individual contributions. Companies changing their systems are trying to figure out how their new practices will affect the pay-for-performance model, which none of them have explicitly abandoned.

They still differentiate rewards, usually relying on managers' qualitative judgments rather than numerical ratings. In pilot programs at Juniper Systems and Cargill, supervisors had no difficulty allocating merit-based pay without appraisal scores. In fact, both line managers and HR staff felt that paying closer attention to employee performance throughout the year was likely to make their merit-pay decisions more valid.

But it will be interesting to see whether most supervisors end up reviewing the feedback they've given each employee over the year before determining merit increases. (Deloitte's managers already do this.) If so, might they produce something *like* an annual appraisal score—even though it's more carefully considered? And could that subtly undermine development by shifting managers' focus back to accountability?

Identifying poor performers

Though managers may assume they need appraisals to determine which employees aren't doing their jobs well, the traditional process doesn't *really* help much with that. For starters, individuals' ratings jump around over time. Research shows that last year's performance score predicts only one-third of the variance in this year's score—so it's hard to say that someone simply isn't up to scratch. Plus, HR departments consistently complain that line managers don't use the appraisal process to document poor performers. Even when they do, waiting until the end of the year to flag struggling employees allows failure to go on for too long without intervention.

We've observed that companies that have dropped appraisals are requiring supervisors to immediately identify problem employees. Juniper Systems also formally asks supervisors each quarter to confirm that their subordinates are performing up to company standards. Only 3%, on average, are not, and HR is brought in to address them. Adobe reports that its new system has reduced dismissals, because struggling employees are monitored and coached much more closely.

Still, given how reluctant most managers are to single out failing employees, we can't assume that getting rid of appraisals will make those tough calls any easier. And all the companies we've observed still have "performance improvement plans" for employees identified as needing support. Such plans remain universally problematic, too, partly because many issues that cause poor performance can't be solved by management intervention.

Avoiding legal troubles

Employee relations managers within HR often worry that discrimination charges will spike if their companies stop basing pay increases and promotions on numerical ratings, which seem objective. But appraisals haven't prevented discriminatory practices. Though they force managers to systematically review people's contributions each year, a great deal of discretion (always subject to bias) is built into the process, and considerable evidence shows that supervisors discriminate against some employees by giving them undeservedly low ratings.

Leaders at Gap report that their new practices were driven partly by complaints and research showing that the appraisal process was often biased and ineffective. Frontline workers in retail (disproportionately women and minorities) are especially vulnerable to unfair treatment. Indeed, formal ratings may do more to *reveal* bias than to curb it. If a company has clear appraisal scores and merit-pay indexes, it is easy to see if women and minorities with the same scores as white men are getting fewer or lower pay increases.

All that said, it's not clear that new approaches to performance management will do much to mitigate discrimination either. (See the sidebar "Can You Take Cognitive Bias Out of Assessments?") Gap has found that getting rid of performance scores increased fairness in pay and other decisions, but judgments still have to be made—and there's the possibility of bias in every piece of qualitative information that decision-makers consider.

Managing the feedback firehose

In recent years most HR information systems were built to move annual appraisals online and connect them to pay increases, succession planning, and so forth. They weren't designed to accommodate continuous feedback, which is one reason many employee check-ins consist of oral comments, with no documentation.

The tech world has responded with apps that enable supervisors to give feedback anytime and to record it if desired. At General Electric, the PD@GE app ("PD" stands for "performance development") allows managers to call up notes and materials from prior conversations and summarize that information. Employees can use the app to ask for direction when they need it. IBM has a similar app that adds another feature: It enables employees to give feedback to peers and choose whether the recipient's boss gets a copy. Amazon's

Can You Take Cognitive Bias Out of Assessments?

A CLASSIC STUDY by Edward Jones and Victor Harris in the 1960s demonstrated that people tend to attribute others' behavior to character rather than circumstances.

When a car goes streaking past us, for instance, we think that the driver is a jerk and ignore the possibility that there might be an emergency. A good workplace example of this cognitive bias—known as the "fundamental attribution error"—is to assume that the lowest performers in any year will always be the worst performers and to fire them as a result. Such an assumption overlooks the impact of good or poor management, not to mention business conditions that are beyond employees' control.

Of course, this model is highly flattering to people who have advanced into executive roles—"A" players whose success is, by definition, credited to their superior abilities, not to good fortune. That may be partly why the model has persisted so long in the face of considerable evidence against it.

Even when "A" players seem to perform well in many contexts (and that's rarely measured), they may be coasting on the "halo effect"—another type of bias, akin to self-fulfilling prophecy. If these folks have already been successful, they receive more opportunities than others, and they're pushed harder, so naturally they do better.

Biases color individual performance ratings as well. Decision-makers may give past behavior too much weight, for instance, or fall prey to stereotypes when they assign their ratings.

But when you get rid of forced ranking and appraisal scores, you don't eradicate bias. Discrimination and faulty assumptions still creep into qualitative assessments. In some ways the older, more cumbersome performance systems actually made it harder for managers to keep their blinders on. Formal feedback from various stakeholders provided some balance when supervisors were otherwise inclined to see only the good things their stars did and failed to recognize others' contributions.

Anytime you exercise judgment, whether or not you translate that to numerical ratings, intuition plays a part, and bias can rear its head.

Anytime Feedback tool does much the same thing. The great advantage of these apps is that supervisors can easily review all the discussion text when it is time to take actions such as award merit pay or consider promotions and job reassignments.

Of course, being on the receiving end of all that continual coaching could get overwhelming—it never lets up. And as for peer feedback, it isn't always useful, even if apps make it easier to deliver in real time. Typically, it's less objective than supervisor feedback, as anyone familiar with 360s knows. It can be also "gamed" by employees to help or hurt colleagues. (At Amazon, the cutthroat culture encourages employees to be critical of one another's performance, and forced ranking creates an incentive to push others to the bottom of the heap.) The more consequential the peer feedback, the more likely the problems.

Not all employers face the same business pressures to change their performance processes. In some fields and industries (think sales and financial services), it still makes sense to emphasize accountability and financial rewards for individual performers. Organizations with a strong public mission may also be well served by traditional appraisals. But even government organizations like NASA and the FBI are rethinking their approach, having concluded that accountability should be collective and that supervisors need to do a better job of coaching and developing their subordinates.

Ideology at the top matters. Consider what happened at Intel. In a two-year pilot, employees got feedback but no formal appraisal scores. Though supervisors did not have difficulty differentiating performance or distributing performance-based pay without the ratings, company executives returned to using them, believing they created healthy competition and clear outcomes. At Sun Communities, a manufactured-home company, senior leaders also oppose eliminating appraisals because they think formal feedback is essential to accountability. And Medtronic, which gave up ratings several years ago, is resurrecting them now that it has acquired

Ireland-based Covidien, which has a more traditional view of performance management.

Other firms aren't completely reverting to old approaches but instead seem to be seeking middle ground. As we've mentioned, Deloitte has backpedaled from giving no ratings at all to having project leads and managers assign them in four categories on a quarterly basis, to provide detailed "performance snapshots." PwC recently made a similar move in its client-services practices: Employees still don't receive a single rating each year, but they now get scores on five competencies, along with other development feedback. In PwC's case, the pushback against going numberless actually came from employees, especially those on a partner track, who wanted to know how they were doing.

At one insurance company, after formal ratings had been eliminated, merit-pay increases were being shared internally and then interpreted as performance scores. These became known as "shadow ratings," and because they started to affect other talent management decisions, the company eventually went back to formal appraisals. But it kept other changes it had made to its performance management system, such as quarterly conversations between managers and employees, to maintain its new commitment to development.

It will be interesting to see how well these "third way" approaches work. They, too, could fail if they aren't supported by senior leadership and reinforced by organizational culture. Still, in most cases, sticking with old systems seems like a bad option. Companies that don't think an overhaul makes sense for them should at least carefully consider whether their process is giving them what they need to solve current performance problems and develop future talent. Performance appraisals wouldn't be the least popular practice in business, as they're widely believed to be, if *something* weren't fundamentally wrong with them.

Originally published in October 2016. Reprint R1610D

Reinventing Performance Management

by Marcus Buckingham and Ashley Goodall

AT DELOITTE WE'RE REDESIGNING our performance management system. This may not surprise you. Like many other companies, we realize that our current process for evaluating the work of our people—and then training them, promoting them, and paying them accordingly—is increasingly out of step with our objectives. In a public survey Deloitte conducted recently, more than half the executives questioned (58%) believe that their current performance management approach drives neither employee engagement nor high performance. They, and we, are in need of something nimbler, real-time, and more individualized—something squarely focused on fueling performance in the future rather than assessing it in the past.

What might surprise you, however, is what we'll include in Deloitte's new system and what we won't. It will have no cascading objectives, no once-a-year reviews, and no 360-degree-feedback tools. We've arrived at a very different and much simpler design for managing people's performance. Its hallmarks are speed, agility, one-size-fits-one, and constant learning, and it's underpinned by a new way of collecting reliable performance data. This system will make much more sense for our talent-dependent business. But we might never have arrived at its design without drawing on three pieces of evidence: a simple counting of hours, a review of research in the science of ratings, and a carefully controlled study of our own organization.

Counting and the Case for Change

More than likely, the performance management system Deloitte has been using has some characteristics in common with yours. Objectives are set for each of our 65,000-plus people at the beginning of the year; after a project is finished, each person's manager rates him or her on how well those objectives were met. The manager also comments on where the person did or didn't excel. These evaluations are factored into a single year-end rating, arrived at in lengthy "consensus meetings" at which groups of "counselors" discuss hundreds of people in light of their peers.

Internal feedback demonstrates that our people like the predictability of this process and the fact that because each person is assigned a counselor, he or she has a representative at the consensus meetings. The vast majority of our people believe the process is fair. We realize, however, that it's no longer the best design for Deloitte's emerging needs: Once-a-year goals are too "batched" for a real-time world, and conversations about year-end ratings are generally less valuable than conversations conducted in the moment about actual performance.

But the need for change didn't crystallize until we decided to count things. Specifically, we tallied the number of hours the organization was spending on performance management—and found that completing the forms, holding the meetings, and creating the ratings consumed close to *2 million hours a year.* As we studied how those hours were spent, we realized that many of them were eaten up by leaders' discussions behind closed doors about the outcomes of the process. We wondered if we could somehow shift our investment of time from talking to ourselves about ratings to talking to our people about their performance and careers—from a focus on the past to a focus on the future.

The Science of Ratings

Our next discovery was that assessing someone's *skills* produces inconsistent data. Objective as I may try to be in evaluating you on, say, strategic thinking, it turns out that how much strategic thinking *I* do, or how valuable *I* think strategic thinking is, or how tough

Idea in Brief

The Problem

Not just employees but their managers and even HR departments are by now questioning the conventional wisdom of performance management, including its common reliance on cascading objectives, backward-looking assessments, once-a-year rankings and reviews, and 360-degree-feedback tools.

The Goal

Some companies have ditched the rankings and even annual reviews, but they haven't found better solutions. Deloitte resolved to design a system that would fairly recognize varying performance, have a clear view into performance anytime, and boost performance in the future.

The Solution

Deloitte's new approach separates compensation decisions from day-to-day performance management, produces better insight through quarterly or per-project "performance snapshots," and relies on weekly check-ins with managers to keep performance on course.

a rater *I* am significantly affects my assessment of *your* strategic thinking.

How significantly? The most comprehensive research on what ratings actually measure was conducted by Michael Mount, Steven Scullen, and Maynard Goff and published in the *Journal of Applied Psychology* in 2000. Their study—in which 4,492 managers were rated on certain performance dimensions by two bosses, two peers, and two subordinates—revealed that 62% of the variance in the ratings could be accounted for by individual raters' peculiarities of perception. Actual performance accounted for only 21% of the variance. This led the researchers to conclude (in *How People Evaluate Others in Organizations,* edited by Manuel London): "Although it is implicitly assumed that the ratings measure the performance of the ratee, most of what is being measured by the ratings is the unique rating tendencies of the rater. Thus ratings reveal more about the rater than they do about the ratee." This gave us pause. We wanted to understand performance at the individual level, and we knew that the person in the best position to judge it was the immediate team leader. But how could we capture a team leader's view of performance without running afoul of what the researchers termed "idiosyncratic rater effects"?

Putting Ourselves Under the Microscope

We also learned that the defining characteristic of the very best teams at Deloitte is that they are strengths oriented. Their members feel that they are called upon to do their best work every day. This discovery was not based on intuitive judgment or gleaned from anecdotes and hearsay; rather, it was derived from an empirical study of our own high-performing teams.

Our study built on previous research. Starting in the late 1990s, Gallup performed a multiyear examination of high-performing teams that eventually involved more than 1.4 million employees, 50,000 teams, and 192 organizations. Gallup asked both high- and lower-performing teams questions on numerous subjects, from mission and purpose to pay and career opportunities, and isolated the questions on which the high-performing teams strongly agreed and the rest did not. It found at the beginning of the study that almost all the variation between high- and lower-performing teams was explained by a very small group of items. The most powerful one proved to be "At work, I have the opportunity to do what I do best every day." Business units whose employees chose "strongly agree" for this item were 44% more likely to earn high customer satisfaction scores, 50% more likely to have low employee turnover, and 38% more likely to be productive.

We set out to see whether those results held at Deloitte. First we identified 60 high-performing teams, which involved 1,287 employees and represented all parts of the organization. For the control group, we chose a representative sample of 1,954 employees. To measure the conditions within a team, we employed a six-item survey. When the results were in and tallied, three items correlated best with high performance for a team: "My coworkers are committed to doing quality work," "The mission of our company inspires me," and "I have the chance to use my strengths every day." Of these, the third was the most powerful across the organization.

All this evidence helped bring into focus the problem we were trying to solve with our new design. We wanted to spend more time helping our people use their strengths—in teams characterized by great clarity of purpose and expectations—and we wanted a quick way to collect reliable and differentiated performance data. With this in mind, we set to work.

Radical Redesign

We began by stating as clearly as we could what performance management is actually *for,* at least as far as Deloitte is concerned. We articulated three objectives for our new system. The first was clear: It would allow us to *recognize* performance, particularly through variable compensation. Most current systems do this.

But to recognize each person's performance, we had to be able to *see* it clearly. That became our second objective. Here we faced two issues—the idiosyncratic rater effect and the need to streamline our traditional process of evaluation, project rating, consensus meeting, and final rating. The solution to the former requires a subtle shift in our approach. Rather than asking more people for their opinion of a team member (in a 360-degree or an upward-feedback survey, for example), we found that we will need to ask only the immediate team leader—but, critically, to ask a different kind of question. People may rate other people's skills inconsistently, but they are highly consistent when rating their own feelings and intentions. To see performance at the individual level, then, we will ask team leaders not about the *skills* of each team member but about their *own future actions* with respect to that person.

At the end of every project (or once every quarter for long-term projects) we will ask team leaders to respond to four future-focused statements about each team member. We've refined the wording of these statements through successive tests, and we know that at Deloitte they clearly highlight differences among individuals and reliably measure performance. Here are the four:

1. Given what I know of this person's performance, and if it were my money, I would award this person the highest possible compensation increase and bonus [*measures overall performance and unique value to the organization on a five-point scale from "strongly agree" to "strongly disagree"*].

2. Given what I know of this person's performance, I would always want him or her on my team [*measures ability to work well with others on the same five-point scale*].

3. This person is at risk for low performance [*identifies problems that might harm the customer or the team on a yes-or-no basis*].

4. This person is ready for promotion today [*measures potential on a yes-or-no basis*].

In effect, we are asking our team leaders what they would *do* with each team member rather than what they *think* of that individual. When we aggregate these data points over a year, weighting each according to the duration of a given project, we produce a rich stream of information for leaders' discussions of what they, in turn, will do—whether it's a question of succession planning, development paths, or performance-pattern analysis. Once a quarter the organization's leaders can use the new data to review a targeted subset of employees (those eligible for promotion, for example, or those with critical skills) and can debate what actions Deloitte might take to better develop that particular group. In this aggregation of simple but powerful data points, we see the possibility of shifting our 2-million-hour annual investment from talking about the ratings to talking about our people—from ascertaining the facts of performance to considering what we should do in response to those facts.

In addition to this consistent—and countable—data, when it comes to compensation, we want to factor in some uncountable things, such as the difficulty of project assignments in a given year and contributions to the organization other than formal projects. So the data will serve as the starting point for compensation, not the ending point. The final determination will be reached either by a leader who knows each individual personally or by a group of leaders looking at an entire segment of our practice and at many data points in parallel.

We could call this new evaluation a rating, but it bears no resemblance, in generation or in use, to the ratings of the past. Because it allows us to quickly capture performance at a single moment in time, we call it a *performance snapshot*.

The Third Objective

Two objectives for our new system, then, were clear: We wanted to recognize performance, and we had to be able to see it clearly. But all our research, all our conversations with leaders on the topic of performance management, and all the feedback from our people left us convinced that something was missing. Is performance management at root more about "management" or about "performance"? Put differently, although it may be great to be able to measure and reward the performance you have, wouldn't it be better still to be able to improve it?

Our third objective therefore became to *fuel* performance. And if the performance snapshot was an organizational tool for measuring it, we needed a tool that team leaders could use to strengthen it.

Research into the practices of the best team leaders reveals that they conduct regular check-ins with each team member about near-term work. These brief conversations allow leaders to set expectations for the upcoming week, review priorities, comment on recent work, and provide course correction, coaching, or important new information. The conversations provide clarity regarding what is expected of each team member and why, what great work looks like, and how each can do his or her best work in the upcoming days—in other words, exactly the trinity of purpose, expectations, and strengths that characterizes our best teams.

Our design calls for every team leader to check in with each team member once a week. For us, these check-ins are not *in addition* to the work of a team leader; they *are* the work of a team leader. If a leader checks in less often than once a week, the team member's priorities may become vague and aspirational, and the leader can't be as helpful—and the conversation will shift from coaching for near-term work to giving feedback about past performance. In other words, the content of these conversations will be a direct outcome of their frequency: If you want people to talk about how to do their best work in the near future, they need to talk often. And so far we have found in our testing a direct and measurable correlation between the frequency of these conversations and the engagement of team

---

Performance intelligence

In an early proof of concept of the redesigned system, executives in one large practice area at Deloitte called up data from project managers to consider important talent-related decisions. In the charts that follow, each dot represents an individual; decision-makers could click on a dot to see the person's name and details from his or her "performance snapshots."

What are team leaders telling us?

*First the group looked at the whole story. This view plotted all the members of the practice according to how much their various project managers agreed with two statements: "I would always want this person on my team" (**y axis**) and "I would give this person the highest possible compensation" (**x axis**). The axes are the same for the other three screens.*

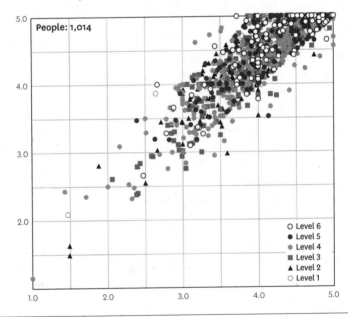

members. Very frequent check-ins (we might say *radically* frequent check-ins) are a team leader's killer app.

That said, team leaders have many demands on their time. We've learned that the best way to ensure frequency is to have check-ins be initiated by the team member—who more often than not is eager for

How would this data help determine pay?

Next the data was filtered to look only at individuals at a given job level. A fundamental question for performance management systems is whether they can capture enough variation among people to fairly allocate pay. A data distribution like this offers a starting point for broader discussion.

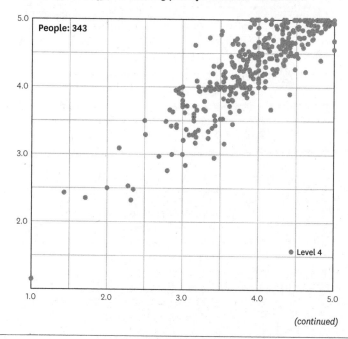

(continued)

the guidance and attention they provide—rather than by the team leader.

To support both people in these conversations, our system will allow individual members to understand and explore their strengths using a self-assessment tool and then to present those strengths to their teammates, their team leader, and the rest of the organization. Our reasoning is twofold. First, as we've seen, people's strengths generate their highest performance today and the greatest improvement in their performance tomorrow, and so deserve to be a central focus. Second, if we want to see frequent (weekly!) use of our system, we have to think of it as a consumer technology—that is, designed to be simple, quick, and above all engaging to use. Many of the successful

How would it help guide promotions?

This view was filtered to show individuals whose team leaders responded "yes" to the statement "This person is ready for promotion today." The data supports objectivity in annual executive discussions about advancement.

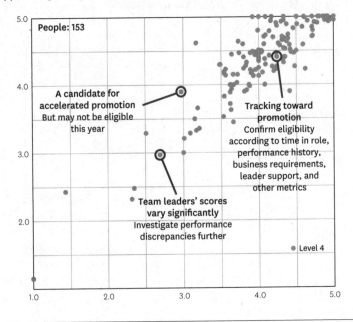

consumer technologies of the past several years (particularly social media) are *sharing* technologies, which suggests that most of us are consistently interested in ourselves—our own insights, achievements, and impact. So we want this new system to provide a place for people to explore and share what is best about themselves.

Transparency

This is where we are today: We've defined three objectives at the root of performance management—to *recognize, see,* and *fuel* performance. We have three interlocking rituals to support them—the annual compensation decision, the quarterly or per-project

How would it help address low performance?

This view was filtered to show individuals whose team leaders responded "yes" to the statement "This person is at risk of low performance." As the upper right of this screen shows, even high performers can slip up—and it's important that the organization help them recover.

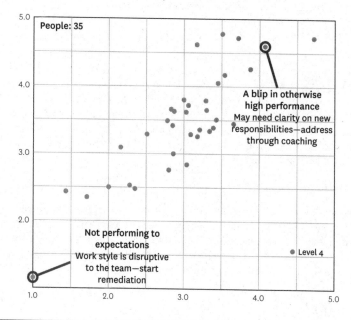

performance snapshot, and the weekly check-in. And we've shifted from a batched focus on the past to a continual focus on the future, through regular evaluations and frequent check-ins. As we've tested each element of this design with ever-larger groups across Deloitte, we've seen that the change can be an evolution over time: Different business units can introduce a strengths orientation first, then more-frequent conversations, then new ways of measuring, and finally new software for monitoring performance. (See the exhibit "Performance intelligence.")

But one issue has surfaced again and again during this work, and that's the issue of transparency. When an organization knows

How Deloitte Built a Radically Simple Performance Measure

ONE OF THE MOST IMPORTANT TOOLS in our redesigned performance management system is the "performance snapshot." It lets us see performance quickly and reliably across the organization, freeing us to spend more time engaging with our people. Here's how we created it.

1. The Criteria

We looked for measures that met three criteria. To neutralize the idiosyncratic rater effect, we wanted raters to rate their own actions, rather than the qualities or behaviors of the ratee. To generate the necessary range, the questions had to be phrased in the extreme. And to avoid confusion, each one had to contain a single, easily understood concept. We chose one about pay, one about teamwork, one about poor performance, and one about promotion. Those categories may or may not be right for other organizations, but they work for us.

2. The Rater

We were looking for someone with vivid experience of the individual's performance and whose subjective judgment we felt was important. We agreed that team leaders are closest to the performance of ratees and, by virtue of their roles, must exercise subjective judgment. We could have included functional managers, or even ratees' peers, but we wanted to start with clarity and simplicity.

3. Testing

We then tested that our questions would produce useful data. Validity testing focuses on their difficulty (as revealed by mean responses) and the

something about us, and that knowledge is captured in a number, we often feel entitled to know it—to know where we stand. We suspect that this issue will need its own radical answer.

In the first version of our design, we kept the results of performance snapshots from the team member. We did this because we knew from the past that when an evaluation is to be shared, the responses skew high—that is, they are sugarcoated. Because we range of responses (as revealed by standard deviations). We knew that if they consistently yielded a tight cluster of "strongly agree" responses, we wouldn't get the differentiation we were looking for. *Construct* validity and *criterion-related* validity are also important. (That is, the questions should collectively test an underlying theory and make it possible to find correlations with outcomes measured in other ways, such as engagement surveys.)

4. Frequency

At Deloitte we live and work in a project structure, so it makes sense for us to produce a performance snapshot at the end of each project. For longer-term projects we've decided that quarterly is the best frequency. Our goal is to strike the right balance between tying the evaluation as tightly as possible to the experience of the performance and not overburdening our team leaders, lest survey fatigue yield poor data.

5. Transparency

We're experimenting with this now. We want our snapshots to reveal the real-time "truth" of what our team leaders think, yet our experience tells us that if they know that team members will see every data point, they may be tempted to sugarcoat the results to avoid difficult conversations. We know that we'll aggregate an individual's snapshot scores into an annual composite. But what, exactly, should we share at year's end? We want to err on the side of sharing more, not less—to aggregate snapshot scores not only for client work but also for internal projects, along with performance metrics such as hours and sales, in the context of a group of peers—so that we can give our people the richest possible view of where they stand. Time will tell how close to that ideal we can get.

wanted to capture unfiltered assessments, we made the responses private. We worried that otherwise we might end up destroying the very truth we sought to reveal.

But what, in fact, is that truth? What do we see when we try to quantify a person? In the world of sports, we have pages of statistics for each player; in medicine, a three-page report each time we get blood work done; in psychometric evaluations, a battery of tests and percentiles. At work, however, at least when it comes to quantifying performance, we try to express the infinite variety and nuance of a human being in a single number.

Surely, however, a better understanding comes from conversations—with your team leader about how you're doing, or between leaders as they consider your compensation or your career. And these conversations are best served not by a single data point but by many. If we want to do our best to tell you where you stand, we must capture as much of your diversity as we can and then talk about it.

We haven't resolved this issue yet, but here's what we're asking ourselves and testing: What's the most detailed view of you that we can gather and share? How does that data support a conversation about your performance? How can we equip our leaders to have insightful conversations? Our question now is not *What is the simplest view of you?* but *What is the richest?*

Over the past few years the debate about performance management has been characterized as a debate about ratings—whether or not they are fair, and whether or not they achieve their stated objectives. But perhaps the issue is different: not so much that ratings fail to convey what the organization knows about each person but that as presented, that knowledge is sadly one-dimensional. In the end, it's not the particular number we assign to a person that's the problem; rather, it's the fact that there *is* a single number. Ratings are a distillation of the truth—and up until now, one might argue, a necessary one. Yet we want our organizations to know us, and we want to know ourselves at work, and that can't be compressed into a single number. We now have the technology to go from a small data version of our people to a big data version of them. As we scale up our new approach across Deloitte, that's the issue we want to solve next.

Originally published in April 2015. Reprint R1504B

Getting 360-Degree Feedback Right

by Maury A. Peiperl

IF A SINGLE EMAIL can send the pulse racing, it's the one from human resources announcing that it's time for another round of 360-degree feedback. In and of itself, this type of appraisal isn't bad. Indeed, many businesspeople would argue that over the past decade, it has revolutionized performance management—for the better. But one aspect of 360-degree feedback consistently stymies executives: peer appraisal. More times than not, it exacerbates bureaucracy, heightens political tensions, and consumes enormous numbers of hours. No wonder so many executives wonder if peer appraisal is worth the effort.

I would argue that it is. Peer appraisal, when conducted effectively, can bolster the overall impact of 360-degree feedback and is as important as feedback from superiors and subordinates. Yet the question remains: can peer appraisal take place without negative side effects? The answer is yes—if executives understand and manage around four inherent paradoxes.

For the past ten years, my research has focused on the theory behind, and practice of, 360-degree feedback. Most recently, I studied its implementation at 17 companies varying in size—from start-ups of a few dozen people to *Fortune* 500 firms—and industry—from high-tech manufacturing to professional services firms. I was looking for answers to several questions. Under what circumstances does peer appraisal improve performance? Why does peer appraisal work well in some cases and fail miserably in others? And finally, how can executives fashion peer appraisal programs to be less anxiety provoking and more productive for the organization?

My research produced a discomforting conclusion: peer appraisal is difficult because it has to be. Four inescapable paradoxes are embedded in the process:

- *The Paradox of Roles:* You cannot be both a peer and a judge.

- *The Paradox of Group Performance:* Focusing on individuals puts the entire group at risk.

- *The Measurement Paradox:* The easier feedback is to gather, the harder it is to apply.

- *The Paradox of Rewards:* When peer appraisal counts the most, it helps the least.

Performance management isn't easy under any circumstances. But a certain clarity exists in the traditional form of performance review, when a boss evaluates a subordinate. The novelty and ambiguity of peer appraisal, on the other hand, give rise to its paradoxes. Fortunately, managers can, with some forward thinking and a deeper understanding of their dynamics, ease the discomfort. Let's consider each paradox in detail.

The Paradox of Roles

Peer appraisal begins with a simple premise: the people best suited to judge the performance of others are those who work most closely with them. In flatter organizations with looser hierarchies, bosses may no longer have all the information they need to appraise subordinates. But it doesn't necessarily follow that peers will eagerly step into the breach. They may tend to give fairly conservative feedback rather than risk straining relationships with colleagues by saying things that could be perceived negatively. Consequently, the feedback gathered from peers may be distorted, overly positive, and, in the end, unhelpful to managers and recipients.

Idea in Brief

Despite how much 360-degree feedback has revolutionized performance management, peer appraisal consistently stymies executives and can exacerbate bureaucracy, heighten political tensions, and consume lots of time. Maury A. Peiperl has studied 360-degree feedback and has asked: under what circumstances does peer appraisal improve performance? Why does peer appraisal sometimes work well and sometimes fail? And how can executives make these programs less anxiety-provoking for participants and more productive for organizations?

Peiperl discusses four paradoxes inherent to peer appraisal:

1. The Paradox of Roles: You cannot be both a peer and a judge.

2. The Paradox of Group Performance: Focusing on individuals puts the entire group at risk.

3. The Measurement Paradox: The easier feedback is to gather, the harder it is to apply.

4. The Paradox of Rewards: When peer appraisal counts the most, it helps the least.

These paradoxes do not have neat solutions, but managers who understand them can better use peer appraisal to improve their organizations.

In more than one team I studied, participants in peer appraisal routinely gave all their colleagues the highest ratings on all dimensions. When I questioned this practice, the responses revealed just how perplexing and risky, both personally and professionally, evaluating peers can be. Some people feared that providing negative feedback would damage relationships and ultimately hurt their own careers and those of their friends and colleagues. Others resisted because they preferred to give feedback informally rather than making it a matter of record. Still other employees resented peer appraisal's playing a part in a performance system that resulted in promotions for some and criticism and even punishment for others—thereby, they believed, compromising the egalitarian and supportive work environments they had tried to cultivate.

When the Paradox of Roles is at play, people are torn between being supportive colleagues or hard-nosed judges. Their natural inclination is to offer counsel and encouragement, and yet they've been asked to pass judgment on a colleague's performance. Unless this conflict is addressed early on, peer appraisal will go nowhere fast—and cause stress and resentment along the way.

The Paradox of Group Performance

Most peer appraisal programs can't reveal what makes a great group tick. Even though such evaluations are intended to gain insights into the workings of teams or groups, peer appraisal programs usually still target individual performance. In most cases, however, a focus on individuals doesn't address how most important work is done these days—that is, through flexible, project-based teams. Moreover, successful groups resent it when management tries to shift their focus or asks them to compare members with one another; in the extreme, peer appraisal may even harm close-knit and successful groups.

In one high-performing group I studied—the venture capital arm of a well-known bank—peer appraisal was roundly viewed as an annoyance of questionable utility. This group was utterly dismissive of the bank's appraisal system, even though the program was well constructed, aggressively backed by top management, and successful in other areas of the bank. The members considered themselves a highly independent group and believed they were already fully aware of their performance, both individually and in project teams. To their way of thinking, they had already created a collegial and cohesive environment that delivered extraordinary results for the company, so why couldn't the bank just leave them alone? The group's finely honed balance of status and responsibilities was threatened by the prospect of individual peer appraisals. Although they halfheartedly participated in one round of 360-degree feedback, over time they simply stopped completing the evaluation forms, thus registering their contempt for (and possibly their fear of) the program.

Low-performing groups also often greet peer appraisal unenthusiastically. At a professional services firm, I met with the partners in charge of a practice that had suffered a long, slow decline in profitability. They saw peer appraisal as a veiled attempt by the rest of the organization to assess blame. As a form of passive protest, this group provided few comments when evaluating one another, and when pressed to discuss results, they resisted. So great was the threat implied by peer appraisal that eventually they refused outright to discuss any feedback they had received, and the process shut down altogether. Their worries about their own failure and the company's motivations became self-fulfilling: As their willingness to discuss results diminished, so did the practice's performance.

As these cases suggest, when peer appraisal ignores group dynamics and work realities, it delivers counterproductive results. If most work is done in groups, focusing on individuals can compromise the group's performance or make a weak team's performance even worse. Rather than cultivating a sense of shared ownership and responsibility, the process can breed deep cynicism, suspicion, and an "us-against-them" mentality—the exact opposite of the values most companies espouse.

The Measurement Paradox

It seems logical that simple, objective, straightforward rating systems should generate the most useful appraisals. Number or letter grades make it easier for managers to gather, aggregate, and compare ratings across individuals and groups, and they often just *seem* like the right way to proceed (after all, most of us have been getting report cards since kindergarten). But ratings by themselves don't yield the detailed, qualitative comments and insights that can help a colleague improve performance. In fact, the simpler the measures and the fewer dimensions on which an individual is measured, the less useful the evaluation.

One media company I observed was especially proud of its performance measurement program, which involved elaborate rounds of evaluations by peers and bosses. The process culminated in a letter grade for every individual, which was then linked to group, division, and, ultimately, corporate results. Top executives were pleased with this approach because of the links it recognized within and between groups. However, many of the employees expressed frustration, not only because the process required an excessive amount of paperwork but also because the system lacked a mechanism for giving or getting detailed feedback beyond a letter grade. Employees frequently reported satisfaction with their ratings, but they complained that they lacked a clear sense of what they had done to deserve their grades and, more important, what they were doing wrong and needed to address in order to progress in their careers. "It's comforting to know I'm an A-plus," one person reported, "but where do I go from here?"

Simple ratings are not always bad, but most of the time they are not enough. Of course, qualitative feedback is more difficult and time-consuming to generate and is not as easily compared and aggregated. It can pose problems of interpretation when comments are personal or highly idiosyncratic (such as, "She is the class of the outfit."). But without specific comments, recipients are left with no information to act on and with little sense of what might help them get better at their jobs.

The Paradox of Rewards

Most people are keenly attuned to peer appraisal when it affects salary reviews and promotions. In the short term, employees may take steps to improve performance (a perpetual latecomer may start showing up on time). But most people focus virtually all their attention on reward outcomes ("Am I going to get a raise or not?"), ignoring the more constructive feedback that peer appraisal generates. Ironically, it is precisely this overlooked feedback that could help to improve performance. Most people don't deliberately ignore peer appraisal feedback, but even the most confident and successful find it hard to interpret objectively when it is part of the formal reward system. In these instances, peer appraisal poses a threat to feelings of self-worth—not to mention net worth.

Is the solution, then, to take rewards out of the equation? My research suggests that the answer is not nearly so straightforward.

Consider this contradiction: in many organizations I surveyed, raters expressed reservations about providing critical feedback when they knew it would directly influence another's salary. One participant put it, "You could destroy somebody and not even know it." But when I queried recipients of peer appraisal, many reported that they weren't interested in feedback unless it "had teeth." If the results were seen as being for "HR purposes," not "business purposes," recipients were less inclined to take the process seriously; if peer feedback didn't have an impact on rewards, it often wasn't used.

With the Paradox of Rewards, managers find themselves in a catch-22. When rewards are on the line, peer appraisal may generate a lot of activity but usually delivers only short-term improvements in performance from feedback that may be conservative or incomplete. When not tied to rewards, feedback is likely to be more comprehensive (and thus potentially useful) but is not seen as important by recipients, who may delay in addressing it or ignore it altogether.

Managing Through the Paradoxes

As might be expected, these paradoxes do not have neat solutions. They are best seen not as obstacles to be overcome but as features of the appraisal landscape to be managed around or even through. The nature of a paradox isn't easily changed, but the way it is viewed can be. Indeed, one of the most significant findings from my research is the pivotal role that managers play in successful peer appraisal. My field notebooks are full of comments from participants about their managers—some commending bosses for active participation, and others condemning behavior that undermined the process. In too many organizations, I've seen peer appraisal programs sabotaged by managers who let it be known through offhand comments or their own lack of participation that peer appraisal might be well and good for everyone else, but not for them. The best managers, on the other hand, act as constructive critics, role models, and willing participants. (See the sidebar "Managing the 'Peer' in Peer Appraisal.")

My findings also suggest that managers and organizations don't spend enough time asking themselves and conveying to employees

Managing the "Peer" in Peer Appraisal

MOST MANAGERS ARE STILL NOT ACCUSTOMED to giving in-depth, constructive feedback. But by learning how to give feedback better— constructively, specifically, and in a timely manner—and by encouraging others to follow suit, managers themselves become the key ingredient in the peer appraisal process.

- **Go public with your support.** Let it be known that you value peer appraisal, and explicitly describe the benefit you and others have gained as a result of your own participation.

- **Be a counselor and role model.** Meet with subordinates to help them understand the assessments they receive, and engage them in discussions of the appraisals and their interpretation—without letting your own opinions dominate. Demystify the process by being open to feedback and self-improvement and by asking for input from others, including subordinates and peers.

- **Provide training early and often.** Allocate time and resources to help raters and recipients practice giving and receiving feedback. This is best accomplished in small groups and small doses, rather than through big, formal training programs.

- **Put substance before rankings.** Pay attention to and publicize results brought about through the feedback system, such as stronger links between departments, cost-saving innovations, and better information flows. Don't emphasize the success of individuals with high feedback numbers because then people may view 360-degree feedback as a popularity contest rather than a tool for improvement.

- **Let people know when they're not doing peer appraisal well.** Better yet, let their peers tell them. Set high expectations of your own peers and hold them to it. These skills only improve with practice, so scheduling time now and then to role-play with colleagues or trainers is worthwhile.

why peer appraisal is being used. The potential benefits may seem obvious at first, but when the purpose and the scope of peer appraisal are not made explicit, conflict soon takes over.

Purpose
In most cases, the purpose of peer appraisal is to provide timely and useful feedback to help individuals improve their performance.

Detailed, qualitative feedback from peers accompanied by coaching and supportive counseling from a manager are essential. If participants understand the reasons for soliciting this kind of feedback, some of the tension of the Measurement Paradox can be overcome. If, however, the purpose of peer appraisal is simply to check that things are going smoothly and to head off major conflicts, a quick and dirty evaluation using only a few numbers will suffice. In one small organization that used only number ratings, the CEO regularly reviewed all feedback summaries; when any two employees' ratings of each other were unusually negative, he brought them together and helped them address their differences. This practice worked because its purpose was explicit—to catch conflicts before they turned into full-blown crises—and because the CEO's visibility actively mitigated the effects of the Measurement Paradox.

Occasionally, peer appraisal is used to improve ties between groups. In these cases, managers should focus the appraisal effort on the entire group rather than on particular members. When groups themselves realize the need for improved links, the effects of the Paradox of Group Performance may be stemmed. In one situation I witnessed, the sales and operations groups in a large financial services firm were not cooperating, and customer complaints were piling up. The manager invited members of each group to provide anonymous feedback to people in the other group. At first, the feedback was terse and critical, but when each group saw that the company was using the feedback not to reward or punish individuals but to highlight the problems between the two groups, the feedback became more extensive and constructive. Eventually, peer evaluation became a regular channel of communication to identify and resolve conflicts between these groups. In this example, peer appraisal succeeded because it first addressed the real-world conflicts that had led to unmet customer demands; only when participants became accustomed to the process was it folded into the formal reward system, thus decreasing the effects of the Paradox of Rewards.

I have also seen peer appraisal programs introduced as part of larger empowerment programs aimed at distributing authority and responsibility more broadly throughout an organization. In one manufacturing company I studied, a group of factory workers designed its own peer evaluation process. The group already performed multiple roles and functions on the factory floor and took responsibility for hiring, training, and quality control, so it also made sense for the members to take charge of evaluating one another's work. Instead of seeing conflict in the new roles, group members saw peer appraisal as a continuation of the other responsibilities they had assumed. The Paradox of Roles was barely evident.

Scope

Managers also need to be selective about how broadly peer appraisal, and 360-degree programs in general, are used. In the name of inclusion, many organizations feel compelled to roll out these programs everywhere. But democracy is overrated, at least when it comes to peer appraisal. One large financial services firm I studied had great success in solving business process issues across several front-office groups through the judicious use of peer evaluation. The process resulted in widely celebrated improvements and better relations between the front-office groups, so much so that other groups in the company wanted to join in. But when the firm introduced the same program to the additional thousand-plus employees, the program collapsed under its own weight. By trying to provide substantial, but in many cases unnecessary, feedback to all, the company compromised its ability to function.

In choosing rating criteria for peer appraisal, it's also important to remember that all jobs are not the same. A customized evaluation takes longer to develop, but as the Measurement Paradox suggests, such an investment of time and effort is crucial because inappropriate or narrowly defined criteria are difficult for peer evaluators to use and even harder for recipients to apply. Moreover, if participants detect that the system is unlikely to improve their performance or rewards, they are even less likely to actively engage in the process with their peers, as the Paradox of Rewards illustrates.

The Paradox of Group Performance will be less of an issue when the right balance is achieved between evaluating the contributions of individuals and acknowledging the interdependencies and connections within groups and across boundaries. Most organizations are notoriously bad at this, often touting teamwork and group performance while assiduously rewarding only individual outcomes. But in a few groups I studied, where the overall size of the bonus pool, for example, depended on everyone's ability to work together, the tension between individual contributions and group outcomes was kept in check. Practices like this not only diminished the effects of the Paradox of Group Performance but also dampened the effects of the Paradox of Rewards, in part because peer appraisal, while tied to rewards, was only one criterion used to decide them. This middle-ground approach to the Paradox of Rewards can work well when participants trust the integrity of the reward determination process.

In the ten years I have spent observing 360-degree feedback, I have seen a number of organizations gradually develop enough trust and confidence to make the most of peer appraisal without incurring dysfunctional consequences. These organizations recognize that 360-degree feedback systems, and peer appraisal programs in particular, are always works in progress—subject to vulnerabilities, requiring sensitivity to hidden conflicts as much as to tangible results, but nevertheless responsive to thoughtful design and purposeful change. Companies that have success with these programs tend to be open to learning and willing to experiment. They are led by executives who are direct about the expected benefits as well as the challenges and who actively demonstrate support for the process. By laying themselves open to praise and criticism from all directions and inviting others to do the same, they guide their organizations to new capacities for continuous improvement.

Originally published in January 2001. Reprint R0101K

The Set-Up-to-Fail Syndrome

by Jean-François Manzoni and Jean-Louis Barsoux

WHEN AN EMPLOYEE FAILS—or even just performs poorly—managers typically do not blame themselves. The employee doesn't understand the work, a manager might contend. Or the employee isn't driven to succeed, can't set priorities, or won't take direction. Whatever the reason, the problem is assumed to be the employee's fault—and the employee's responsibility.

But is it? Sometimes, of course, the answer is yes. Some employees are not up to their assigned tasks and never will be, for lack of knowledge, skill, or simple desire. But sometimes—and we would venture to say often—an employee's poor performance can be blamed largely on his boss.

Perhaps "blamed" is too strong a word, but it is directionally correct. In fact, our research strongly suggests that bosses—albeit accidentally and usually with the best intentions—are often complicit in an employee's lack of success. (See the sidebar "About the Research.") How? By creating and reinforcing a dynamic that essentially sets up perceived underperformers to fail. If the Pygmalion effect describes the dynamic in which an individual lives up to great expectations, the set-up-to-fail syndrome explains the opposite. It describes a dynamic in which employees perceived to be mediocre or weak performers live down to the low expectations their managers have for them. The result is that they often end up leaving the organization—either of their own volition or not.

The syndrome usually begins surreptitiously. The initial impetus can be performance-related, such as when an employee loses a client, undershoots a target, or misses a deadline. Often, however, the trigger is less specific. An employee is transferred into a division with a lukewarm recommendation from a previous boss. Or perhaps the boss and the employee don't really get along on a personal basis—several studies have indeed shown that compatibility between boss and subordinate, based on similarity of attitudes, values, or social characteristics, can have a significant impact on a boss's impressions. In any case, the syndrome is set in motion when the boss begins to worry that the employee's performance is not up to par.

The boss then takes what seems like the obvious action in light of the subordinate's perceived shortcomings: He increases the time and attention he focuses on the employee. He requires the employee to get approval before making decisions, asks to see more paperwork documenting those decisions, or watches the employee at meetings more closely and critiques his comments more intensely.

These actions are intended to boost performance and prevent the subordinate from making errors. Unfortunately, however, subordinates often interpret the heightened supervision as a lack of trust and confidence. In time, because of low expectations, they come to doubt their own thinking and ability, and they lose the motivation to make autonomous decisions or to take any action at all. The boss, they figure, will just question everything they do—or do it himself anyway.

Ironically, the boss sees the subordinate's withdrawal as proof that the subordinate is indeed a poor performer. The subordinate, after all, isn't contributing his ideas or energy to the organization. So what does the boss do? He increases his pressure and supervision again—watching, questioning, and double-checking everything the subordinate does. Eventually, the subordinate gives up on his dreams of making a meaningful contribution. Boss and subordinate typically settle into a routine that is not really satisfactory but, aside from periodic clashes, is otherwise bearable for them. In the worst-case scenario, the boss's intense intervention and scrutiny end up

Idea in Brief

That darned employee! His performance keeps deteriorating—*despite* your close monitoring. What's going on?

Brace yourself: *You* may be at fault, by unknowingly triggering the **set-up-to-fail syndrome**. Employees whom you (perhaps falsely) view as weak performers live *down* to your expectations. Here's how:

1. You start with a positive relationship.

2. Something—a missed deadline, a lost client—makes you question the employee's performance. You begin micromanaging him.

3. Suspecting your reduced confidence, the employee starts doubting *himself.* He stops giving his best, responds mechanically to your controls, and avoids decisions.

4. You view his new behavior as additional proof of mediocrity—and tighten the screws further.

Why not just fire him? Because you're likely to repeat the pattern with others. Better to *reverse* the dynamic instead. Unwinding the set-up-to-fail spiral actually pays big dividends: Your company gets the best from your employees—and from you.

paralyzing the employee into inaction and consume so much of the boss's time that the employee quits or is fired. (See the exhibit "The set-up-to-fail syndrome.")

Perhaps the most daunting aspect of the set-up-to-fail syndrome is that it is self-fulfilling and self-reinforcing—it is the quintessential vicious circle. The process is self-fulfilling because the boss's actions contribute to the very behavior that is expected from weak performers. It is self-reinforcing because the boss's low expectations, in being fulfilled by his subordinates, trigger more of the same behavior on his part, which in turn triggers more of the same behavior on the part of subordinates. And on and on, unintentionally, the relationship spirals downward.

A case in point is the story of Steve, a manufacturing supervisor for a *Fortune* 100 company. When we first met Steve, he came across as highly motivated, energetic, and enterprising. He was on top of

Idea in Practice

How Set-Up-to-Fail Starts

A manager categorizes employees as "in" or "out," based on:

- early *perceptions* of employees' motivation, initiative, creativity, strategic perspectives;

- previous bosses' impressions;

- an early mishap; and

- boss-subordinate incompatibility.

The manager then notices *only* evidence supporting his categorization, while dismissing contradictory evidence. The boss also treats the groups differently:

- "In" groups get autonomy, feedback, and expressions of confidence.

- "Out" groups get controlling, formal management emphasizing rules.

The Costs of Set-Up-to-Fail

This syndrome hurts everyone:

- *Employees* stop volunteering ideas and information and asking for help, avoid contact with bosses, or grow defensive.

- The *organization* fails to get the most from employees.

- The *boss* loses energy to attend to other activities. His reputation suffers as other employees deem him unfair.

- *Team spirit* wilts as targeted performers are alienated and strong performers are overburdened.

How to Reverse Set-Up-to-Fail

If the syndrome hasn't started, prevent it:

- Establish expectations with new employees early. Loosen

his operation, monitoring problems and addressing them quickly. His boss expressed great confidence in him and gave him an excellent performance rating. Because of his high performance, Steve was chosen to lead a new production line considered essential to the plant's future.

In his new job, Steve reported to Jeff, who had just been promoted to a senior management position at the plant. In the first few weeks of the relationship, Jeff periodically asked Steve to write up short analyses of significant quality-control rejections. Although Jeff didn't really explain this to Steve at the time, his request had two major objectives: to generate information that would help both of them learn the new production process, and to help Steve develop

THE SET-UP-TO-FAIL SYNDROME

the reins as they master their jobs.

- Regularly challenge your own assumptions. Ask: "What are the *facts* regarding this employee's performance?" "Is he really that bad?"

- Convey openness, letting employees challenge your opinions. They'll feel comfortable discussing their performance and relationship with you.

If the syndrome has already erupted, discuss the dynamic with the employee:

1. Choose a neutral, nonthreatening location; use affirming language ("Let's discuss our relationship and roles"); and acknowledge your part in the tension.

2. Agree on the employee's weaknesses and strengths. Support assessments with facts, not feelings.

3. Unearth causes of the weaknesses. Do you disagree on priorities? Does your employee lack specific knowledge or skills? Ask: "How is my behavior making things worse for you?"

4. Identify ways to boost performance. Training? New experiences? Decide the quantity and type of supervision you'll provide. Affirm your desire to improve matters.

5. Agree to communicate more openly: "Next time I do something that communicates low expectations, can you let me know immediately?"

---

the habit of systematically performing root cause analysis of quality-related problems. Also, being new on the job himself, Jeff wanted to show his own boss that he was on top of the operation.

Unaware of Jeff's motives, Steve balked. Why, he wondered, should he submit reports on information he understood and monitored himself? Partly due to lack of time, partly in response to what he considered interference from his boss, Steve invested little energy in the reports. Their tardiness and below-average quality annoyed Jeff, who began to suspect that Steve was not a particularly proactive manager. When he asked for the reports again, he was more forceful. For Steve, this merely confirmed that Jeff did not trust him. He withdrew more and more from interaction with

The set-up-to-fail syndrome

No harm intended: A relationship spirals from bad to worse

1. Before the set-up-to-fail syndrome begins, the boss and the subordinate are typically engaged in a positive, or at least neutral, relationship.

2. The triggering event in the set-up-to-fail syndrome is often minor or surreptitious. The subordinate may miss a deadline, lose a client, or submit a subpar report. In other cases, the syndrome's genesis is the boss, who distances himself from the subordinate for personal or social reasons unrelated to performance.

3. Reacting to the triggering event, the boss increases his supervision of the subordinate, gives more specific instructions, and wrangles longer over courses of action.

4. The subordinate responds by beginning to suspect a lack of confidence and senses he's not part of the boss's in-group anymore.
   He starts to withdraw emotionally from the boss and from work. He may also fight to change the boss's image of him, reaching too high or running too fast to be effective.

5. The boss interprets this problem-hoarding, overreaching, or tentativeness as signs that the subordinate has poor judgment and weak capabilities. If the subordinate does perform well, the boss does not acknowledge it or considers it a lucky one-off.
   He limits the subordinate's discretion, withholds social contact, and shows, with increasing openness, his lack of confidence in and frustration with the subordinate.

6. The subordinate feels boxed in and underappreciated. He increasingly withdraws from his boss and from work. He may even resort to ignoring instructions, openly disputing the boss, and occasionally lashing out because of feelings of rejection.
   In general, he performs his job mechanically and devotes more energy to self-protection. Moreover, he refers all nonroutine decisions to the boss or avoids contact with him.

7. The boss feels increasingly frustrated and is now convinced that the subordinate cannot perform without intense oversight. He makes this known by his words and deeds, further undermining the subordinate's confidence and prompting inaction.

8. When the set-up-to-fail syndrome is in full swing, the boss pressures and controls the subordinate during interactions. Otherwise, he avoids contact and gives the subordinate routine assignments only.
   For his part, the subordinate shuts down or leaves, either in dismay, frustration, or anger.

him, meeting his demands with increased passive resistance. Before long, Jeff became convinced that Steve was not effective enough and couldn't handle his job without help. He started to supervise Steve's every move—to Steve's predictable dismay. One year after excitedly taking on the new production line, Steve was so dispirited he was thinking of quitting.

About the Research

THIS ARTICLE IS BASED on two studies designed to understand better the causal relationship between leadership style and subordinate performance—in other words, to explore how bosses and subordinates mutually influence each other's behavior. The first study, which comprised surveys, interviews, and observations, involved 50 boss-subordinate pairs in four manufacturing operations in *Fortune* 100 companies. The second study, involving an informal survey of about 850 senior managers attending INSEAD executive-development programs over the last three years, was done to test and refine the findings generated by the first study. The executives in the second study represented a wide diversity of nationalities, industries, and personal backgrounds.

How can managers break the set-up-to-fail syndrome? Before answering that question, let's take a closer look at the dynamics that set the syndrome in motion and keep it going.

Deconstructing the Syndrome

We said earlier that the set-up-to-fail syndrome usually starts surreptitiously—that is, it is a dynamic that usually creeps up on the boss and the subordinate until suddenly both of them realize that the relationship has gone sour. But underlying the syndrome are several assumptions about weaker performers that bosses appear to accept uniformly. Our research shows, in fact, that executives typically compare weaker performers with stronger performers using the following descriptors:

- less motivated, less energetic, and less likely to go beyond the call of duty;

- more passive when it comes to taking charge of problems or projects;

- less aggressive about anticipating problems;

- less innovative and less likely to suggest ideas;

53

- more parochial in their vision and strategic perspective;

- more prone to hoard information and assert their authority, making them poor bosses to their own subordinates.

It is not surprising that on the basis of these assumptions, bosses tend to treat weaker and stronger performers very differently. Indeed, numerous studies have shown that up to 90% of all managers treat some subordinates as though they were members of an in-group, while they consign others to membership in an out-group. Members of the in-group are considered the trusted collaborators and therefore receive more autonomy, feedback, and expressions of confidence from their bosses. The boss-subordinate relationship for this group is one of mutual trust and reciprocal influence. Members of the out-group, on the other hand, are regarded more as hired hands and are managed in a more formal, less personal way, with more emphasis on rules, policies, and authority. (For more on how bosses treat weaker and stronger performers differently, see the chart "In with the in crowd, out with the out.")

Why do managers categorize subordinates into either in-groups or out-groups? For the same reason that we tend to typecast our family, friends, and acquaintances: It makes life easier. Labeling is something we all do, because it allows us to function more efficiently. It saves time by providing rough-and-ready guides for interpreting events and interacting with others. Managers, for instance, use categorical thinking to figure out quickly who should get what tasks. That's the good news.

The downside of categorical thinking is that in organizations it leads to premature closure. Having made up his mind about a subordinate's limited ability and poor motivation, a manager is likely to notice supporting evidence while selectively dismissing contrary evidence. (For example, a manager might interpret a terrific new product idea from an out-group subordinate as a lucky onetime event.) Unfortunately for some subordinates, several studies show that bosses tend to make decisions about in-groups and out-groups even as early as five days into their relationships with employees.

In with the in crowd, out with the out

Boss's behavior toward perceived stronger performers	Boss's behavior toward perceived weaker performers
Discusses project objectives, with a limited focus on project implementation. Gives subordinate the freedom to choose his own approach to solving problems or reaching goals.	Is directive when discussing tasks and goals. Focuses on what needs to get done as well as how it should get done.
Treats unfavorable variances, mistakes, or incorrect judgments as learning opportunities.	Pays close attention to unfavorable variances, mistakes, or incorrect judgments.
Makes himself available, as in "let me know if I can help." Initiates casual and personal conversations.	Makes himself available to subordinate on a need-to-see basis. Bases conversations primarily on work-related topics.
Is open to subordinate's suggestions and discusses them with interest.	Pays little interest to subordinate's comments or suggestions about how and why work is done.
Gives subordinate interesting and challenging stretch assignments. Often allows subordinate to choose his own assignments.	Reluctantly gives subordinate anything but routine assignments. When handing out assignments, gives subordinate little choice. Monitors subordinate heavily.
Solicits opinions from subordinate on organizational strategy, execution, policy, and procedures.	Rarely asks subordinate for input about organizational or work-related matters.
Often defers to subordinate's opinion in disagreements.	Usually imposes own views in disagreements.
Praises subordinate for work well done.	Emphasizes what the subordinate is doing poorly.

Are bosses aware of this sorting process and of their different approaches to "in" and "out" employees? Definitely. In fact, the bosses we have studied, regardless of nationality, company, or personal background, were usually quite conscious of behaving in a more controlling way with perceived weaker performers. Some of them preferred to label this approach as "supportive and helpful." Many of them also acknowledged that—although they tried not to— they tended to become impatient with weaker performers more easily than with stronger performers. By and large, however, managers are aware of the controlling nature of their behavior toward perceived weaker performers. For them, this behavior is not an error in implementation; it is intentional.

What bosses typically do *not* realize is that their tight controls end up hurting subordinates' performance by undermining their motivation in two ways: first, by depriving subordinates of autonomy on the job and, second, by making them feel undervalued. Tight controls are an indication that the boss assumes the subordinate can't perform well without strict guidelines. When the subordinate senses these low expectations, it can undermine his self-confidence. This is particularly problematic because numerous studies confirm that people perform up or down to the levels their bosses expect from them or, indeed, to the levels they expect from themselves.[1]

Of course, executives often tell us, "Oh, but I'm very careful about this issue of expectations. I exert more control over my underperformers, but I make sure that it does not come across as a lack of trust or confidence in their ability." We believe what these executives tell us. That is, we believe that they do try hard to disguise their intentions. When we talk to their subordinates, however, we find that these efforts are for the most part futile. In fact, our research shows that most employees can—and do—"read their boss's mind." In particular, they know full well whether they fit into their boss's in-group or out-group. All they have to do is compare how they are treated with how their more highly regarded colleagues are treated.

Just as the boss's assumptions about weaker performers and the right way to manage them explains his complicity in the set-up-to-fail syndrome, the subordinate's assumptions about what the boss is thinking explain his own complicity. The reason? When people perceive disapproval, criticism, or simply a lack of confidence and appreciation, they tend to shut down—a behavioral phenomenon that manifests itself in several ways.

Primarily, shutting down means disconnecting intellectually and emotionally. Subordinates simply stop giving their best. They grow tired of being overruled, and they lose the will to fight for their ideas. As one subordinate put it, "My boss tells me how to execute every detail. Rather than arguing with him, I've ended up wanting to say, 'Come on, just tell me what you want me to do, and I'll go do it.' You become a robot." Another perceived weak performer explained, "When my boss tells me to do something, I just do it mechanically."

Shutting down also involves disengaging personally—essentially reducing contact with the boss. Partly, this disengagement is motivated by the nature of previous exchanges that have tended to be negative in tone. As one subordinate admitted, "I used to initiate much more contact with my boss until the only thing I received was negative feedback; then I started shying away."

Besides the risk of a negative reaction, perceived weaker performers are concerned with not tainting their images further. Following the often-heard aphorism "Better to keep quiet and look like a fool than to open your mouth and prove it," they avoid asking for help for fear of further exposing their limitations. They also tend to volunteer less information—a simple "heads up" from a perceived underperformer can cause the boss to overreact and jump into action when none is required. As one perceived weak performer recalled, "I just wanted to let my boss know about a small matter, only slightly out of the routine, but as soon as I mentioned it, he was all over my case. I should have kept my mouth closed. I do now."

Finally, shutting down can mean becoming defensive. Many perceived underperformers start devoting more energy to self-justification. Anticipating that they will be personally blamed for failures, they seek to find excuses early. They end up spending a lot of time looking in the rearview mirror and less time looking at the road ahead. In some cases—as in the case of Steve, the manufacturing supervisor described earlier—this defensiveness can lead to non-compliance or even systematic opposition to the boss's views. While this idea of a weak subordinate going head to head with his boss may seem irrational, it may reflect what Albert Camus once observed: "When deprived of choice, the only freedom left is the freedom to say no."

The Syndrome Is Costly

There are two obvious costs of the set-up-to-fail syndrome: the emotional cost paid by the subordinate and the organizational cost associated with the company's failure to get the best out of an employee. Yet there are other costs to consider, some of them indirect and long term.

The boss pays for the syndrome in several ways. First, uneasy relationships with perceived low performers often sap the boss's emotional and physical energy. It can be quite a strain to keep up a facade of courtesy and pretend everything is fine when both parties know it is not. In addition, the energy devoted to trying to fix these relationships or improve the subordinate's performance through increased supervision prevents the boss from attending to other activities—which often frustrates or even angers the boss.

Furthermore, the syndrome can take its toll on the boss's reputation, as other employees in the organization observe his behavior toward weaker performers. If the boss's treatment of a subordinate is deemed unfair or unsupportive, observers will be quick to draw their lessons. One outstanding performer commented on his boss's controlling and hypercritical behavior toward another subordinate: "It made us all feel like we're expendable." As organizations increasingly espouse the virtues of learning and empowerment, managers must cultivate their reputations as coaches, as well as get results.

The set-up-to-fail syndrome also has serious consequences for any team. A lack of faith in perceived weaker performers can tempt bosses to overload those whom they consider superior performers; bosses want to entrust critical assignments to those who can be counted on to deliver reliably and quickly and to those who will go beyond the call of duty because of their strong sense of shared fate. As one boss half-jokingly said, "Rule number one: If you want something done, give it to someone who's busy—there's a reason why that person is busy."

An increased workload may help perceived superior performers learn to manage their time better, especially as they start to delegate to their own subordinates more effectively. In many cases, however, these performers simply absorb the greater load and higher stress which, over time, takes a personal toll and decreases the attention they can devote to other dimensions of their jobs, particularly those yielding longer-term benefits. In the worst-case scenario, overburdening strong performers can lead to burnout.

Team spirit can also suffer from the progressive alienation of one or more perceived low performers. Great teams share a sense of enthusiasm and commitment to a common mission. Even when members of the boss's out-group try to keep their pain to themselves, other team members feel the strain. One manager recalled the discomfort experienced by the whole team as they watched their boss grill one of their peers every week. As he explained, "A team is like a functioning organism. If one member is suffering, the whole team feels that pain."

In addition, alienated subordinates often do not keep their suffering to themselves. In the corridors or over lunch, they seek out sympathetic ears to vent their recriminations and complaints, not only wasting their own time but also pulling their colleagues away from productive work. Instead of focusing on the team's mission, valuable time and energy is diverted to the discussion of internal politics and dynamics.

Finally, the set-up-to-fail syndrome has consequences for the subordinates of the perceived weak performers. Consider the weakest kid in the school yard who gets pummeled by a bully. The abused child often goes home and pummels his smaller, weaker siblings. So it is with the people who are in the boss's out-group. When they have to manage their own employees, they frequently replicate the behavior that their bosses show to them. They fail to recognize good results or, more often, supervise their employees excessively.

Breaking Out Is Hard to Do

The set-up-to-fail syndrome is not irreversible. Subordinates can break out of it, but we have found that to be rare. The subordinate must consistently deliver such superior results that the boss is forced to change the employee from out-group to in-group status—a phenomenon made difficult by the context in which these subordinates operate. It is hard for subordinates to impress their bosses when they must work on unchallenging tasks, with no autonomy and limited resources; it is also hard for them to persist and maintain high standards when they receive little encouragement from their bosses.

Furthermore, even if the subordinate achieves better results, it may take some time for them to register with the boss because of his selective observation and recall. Indeed, research shows that bosses tend to attribute the good things that happen to weaker performers to external factors rather than to their efforts and ability (while the opposite is true for perceived high performers: Successes tend to be seen as theirs, and failures tend to be attributed to external uncontrollable factors). The subordinate will therefore need to achieve a string of successes in order to have the boss even contemplate revising the initial categorization. Clearly, it takes a special kind of courage, self-confidence, competence, and persistence on the part of the subordinate to break out of the syndrome.

Instead, what often happens is that members of the out-group set excessively ambitious goals for themselves to impress the boss quickly and powerfully—promising to hit a deadline three weeks early, for instance, or attacking six projects at the same time, or simply attempting to handle a large problem without help. Sadly, such superhuman efforts are usually just that. And in setting goals so high that they are bound to fail, the subordinates also come across as having had very poor judgment in the first place.

The set-up-to-fail syndrome is not restricted to incompetent bosses. We have seen it happen to people perceived within their organizations to be excellent bosses. Their mismanagement of some subordinates need not prevent them from achieving success, particularly when they and the perceived superior performers achieve high levels of individual performance. However, those bosses could be even more successful to the team, the organization, and themselves if they could break the syndrome.

Getting It Right

As a general rule, the first step in solving a problem is recognizing that one exists. This observation is especially relevant to the set-up-to-fail syndrome because of its self-fulfilling and self-reinforcing nature. Interrupting the syndrome requires that a manager understand the dynamic and, particularly, that he accept the possibility that his own behavior may be contributing to a subordinate's under-performance. The next step toward cracking the syndrome, however, is more difficult: It requires a carefully planned and structured intervention that takes the form of one (or several) candid conversations meant to bring to the surface and untangle the unhealthy dynamics that define the boss and the subordinate's relationship. The goal of such an intervention is to bring about a sustainable increase in the subordinate's performance while progressively reducing the boss's involvement.

It would be difficult—and indeed, detrimental—to provide a detailed script of what this kind of conversation should sound like. A boss who rigidly plans for this conversation with a subordinate will not be able to engage in real dialogue with him, because real dialogue requires flexibility. As a guiding framework, however, we offer five components that characterize effective interventions. Although they are not strictly sequential steps, all five components should be part of these interventions.

First, the boss must create the right context for the discussion

He must, for instance, select a time and place to conduct the meeting so that it presents as little threat as possible to the subordinate. A neutral location may be more conducive to open dialogue than an office where previous and perhaps unpleasant conversations have taken place. The boss must also use affirming language when asking the subordinate to meet with him. The session should not be billed as "feedback," because such terms may suggest baggage from the past. "Feedback" could also be taken to mean that the conversation will be one-directional, a monologue delivered by the boss to the subordinate. Instead, the intervention should be described as a meeting to discuss the performance of the subordinate, the role of the boss, and the relationship between the subordinate and the boss. The boss might even acknowledge that he feels tension in the relationship and wants to use the conversation as a way to decrease it.

Finally, in setting the context, the boss should tell the perceived weaker performer that he would genuinely like the interaction to be an open dialogue. In particular, he should acknowledge that he may be partially responsible for the situation and that his own behavior toward the subordinate is fair game for discussion.

Second, the boss and the subordinate must use the intervention process to come to an agreement on the symptoms of the problem

Few employees are ineffective in all aspects of their performance. And few—if any—employees desire to do poorly on the job. Therefore, it is critical that the intervention result in a mutual understanding of the specific job responsibilities in which the subordinate is weak. In the case of Steve and Jeff, for instance, an exhaustive sorting of the evidence might have led to an agreement that Steve's underperformance was not universal but instead largely confined to the quality of the reports he submitted (or failed to submit). In another situation, it might be agreed that a purchasing manager was weak when it came to finding off-shore suppliers and to voicing his ideas in meetings. Or a new investment professional and his boss might come to agree that his performance was subpar when it came to timing the sales and purchase of stocks, but they might also agree that his financial analysis of stocks was quite strong. The idea here is that before working to improve performance or reduce tension in a relationship, an agreement must be reached about what areas of performance contribute to the contentiousness.

We used the word "evidence" above in discussing the case of Steve and Jeff. That is because a boss needs to back up his performance assessments with facts and data—that is, if the intervention is to be useful. They cannot be based on feelings—as in Jeff telling Steve, "I just have the feeling you're not putting enough energy into the reports." Instead, Jeff needs to describe what a good report should look like and the ways in which Steve's reports fall short. Likewise, the subordinate must be allowed—indeed, encouraged—to defend his performance, compare it with colleagues' work, and point out areas in which he is strong. After all, just because it is the boss's opinion does not make it a fact.

**Third, the boss and the subordinate should arrive at
a common understanding of what might be causing
the weak performance in certain areas**

Once the areas of weak performance have been identified, it is time
to unearth the reasons for those weaknesses. Does the subordinate
have limited skills in organizing work, managing his time, or working with others? Is he lacking knowledge or capabilities? Do the boss
and the subordinate agree on their priorities? Maybe the subordinate
has been paying less attention to a particular dimension of his work
because he does not realize its importance to the boss. Does the subordinate become less effective under pressure? Does he have lower
standards for performance than the boss does?

It is also critical in the intervention that the boss bring up the subject of his own behavior toward the subordinate and how this affects
the subordinate's performance. The boss might even try to describe
the dynamics of the set-up-to-fail syndrome. "Does my behavior
toward you make things worse for you?" he might ask, or, "What am
I doing that is leading you to feel that I am putting too much pressure
on you?"

This component of the discussion also needs to make explicit the
assumptions that the boss and the subordinate have thus far been
making about each other's intentions. Many misunderstandings
start with untested assumptions. For example, Jeff might have said,
"When you did not supply me with the reports I asked for, I came to
the conclusion that you were not very proactive." That would have
allowed Steve to bring his buried assumptions into the open. "No," he
might have answered, "I just reacted negatively because you asked
for the reports in writing, which I took as a sign of excessive control."

**Fourth, the boss and the subordinate should arrive at
an agreement about their performance objectives and
on their desire to have the relationship move forward**

In medicine, a course of treatment follows the diagnosis of an illness. Things are a bit more complex when repairing organizational
dysfunction, since modifying behavior and developing complex

skills can be more difficult than taking a few pills. Still, the principle that applies to medicine also applies to business: Boss and subordinate must use the intervention to plot a course of treatment regarding the root problems they have jointly identified.

The contract between boss and subordinate should identify the ways they can improve on their skills, knowledge, experience, or personal relationship. It should also include an explicit discussion of how much and what type of future supervision the boss will have. No boss, of course, should suddenly abdicate his involvement; it is legitimate for bosses to monitor subordinates' work, particularly when a subordinate has shown limited abilities in one or more facets of his job. From the subordinate's point of view, however, such involvement by the boss is more likely to be accepted, and possibly even welcomed, if the goal is to help the subordinate develop and improve over time. Most subordinates can accept temporary involvement that is meant to decrease as their performance improves. The problem is intense monitoring that never seems to go away.

Fifth, the boss and the subordinate should agree to communicate more openly in the future

The boss could say, "Next time I do something that communicates low expectations, can you let me know immediately?" And the subordinate might say, or be encouraged to say, "Next time I do something that aggravates you or that you do not understand, can you also let me know right away?" Those simple requests can open the door to a more honest relationship almost instantly.

No Easy Answer

Our research suggests that interventions of this type do not take place very often. Face-to-face discussions about a subordinate's performance tend to come high on the list of workplace situations people would rather avoid, because such conversations have the potential to make both parties feel threatened or embarrassed. Subordinates are reluctant to trigger the discussion because they are worried about coming across as thin-skinned or whiny. Bosses tend to avoid initiating these talks because they are concerned about the way the subordinate might react; the discussion could force the boss to make explicit his lack of confidence in the subordinate, in turn putting the subordinate on the defensive and making the situation worse.[2]

As a result, bosses who observe the dynamics of the set-up-to-fail syndrome being played out may be tempted to avoid an explicit discussion. Instead, they will proceed tacitly by trying to encourage their perceived weak performers. That approach has the short-term benefit of bypassing the discomfort of an open discussion, but it has three major disadvantages.

First, a one-sided approach on the part of the boss is less likely to lead to lasting improvement because it focuses on only one symptom of the problem—the boss's behavior. It does not address the subordinate's role in the underperformance.

Second, even if the boss's encouragement were successful in improving the employee's performance, a unilateral approach would limit what both he and the subordinate could otherwise learn from a more up-front handling of the problem. The subordinate, in particular, would not have the benefit of observing and learning from how his boss handled the difficulties in their relationship—problems the subordinate may come across someday with the people he manages.

Finally, bosses trying to modify their behavior in a unilateral way often end up going overboard; they suddenly give the subordinate more autonomy and responsibility than he can handle productively. Predictably, the subordinate fails to deliver to the boss's satisfaction, which leaves the boss even more frustrated and convinced that the subordinate cannot function without intense supervision.

We are not saying that intervention is always the best course of action. Sometimes, intervention is not possible or desirable. There may be, for instance, overwhelming evidence that the subordinate is not capable of doing his job. He was a hiring or promotion mistake, which is best handled by removing him from the position. In other cases, the relationship between the boss and the subordinate is too far gone—too much damage has occurred to repair it. And finally, sometimes bosses are too busy and under too much pressure to invest the kind of resources that intervention involves.

Yet often the biggest obstacle to effective intervention is the boss's mindset. When a boss believes that a subordinate is a weak performer and, on top of everything else, that person also aggravates him, he is not going to be able to cover up his feelings with words; his underlying convictions will come out in the meeting. That is why preparation for the intervention is crucial. Before even deciding to have a meeting, the boss must separate emotion from reality. Was the situation always as bad as it is now? Is the subordinate really as bad as I think he is? What is the hard evidence I have for that belief? Could there be other factors, aside from performance, that have led me to label this subordinate a weak performer? Aren't there a few things that he does well? He must have displayed above-average qualifications when we decided to hire him. Did these qualifications evaporate all of a sudden?

The boss might even want to mentally play out part of the conversation beforehand. If I say this to the subordinate, what might he answer? Yes, sure, he would say that it was not his fault and that the customer was unreasonable. Those excuses—are they really without merit? Could he have a point? Could it be that, under other circumstances, I might have looked more favorably upon them? And if I still believe I'm right, how can I help the subordinate see things more clearly?

The boss must also mentally prepare himself to be open to the subordinate's views, even if the subordinate challenges him about any evidence regarding his poor performance. It will be easier for the boss to be open if, when preparing for the meeting, he has already challenged his own preconceptions.

Even when well prepared, bosses typically experience some degree of discomfort during intervention meetings. That is not all bad. The subordinate will probably be somewhat uncomfortable as well, and it is reassuring for him to see that his boss is a human being, too.

Calculating Costs and Benefits

As we've said, an intervention is not always advisable. But when it is, it results in a range of outcomes that are uniformly better than the alternative—that is, continued underperformance and tension. After all, bosses who systematically choose either to ignore their subordinates' underperformance or to opt for the more expedient solution of simply removing perceived weak performers are condemned to keep repeating the same mistakes. Finding and training replacements for perceived weak performers is a costly and recurrent expense. So is monitoring and controlling the deteriorating performance of a disenchanted subordinate. Getting results *in spite of* one's staff is not a sustainable solution. In other words, it makes sense to think of the intervention as an investment, not an expense—with the payback likely to be high.

How high that payback will be and what form it will take obviously depend on the outcome of the intervention, which will itself depend not only on the quality of the intervention but also on several key contextual factors: How long has that relationship been spiraling downward? Does the subordinate have the intellectual and emotional resources to make the effort that will be required? Does the boss have enough time and energy to do his part?

We have observed outcomes that can be clustered into three categories. In the best-case scenario, the intervention leads to a mixture of coaching, training, job redesign, and a clearing of the air; as a result, the relationship and the subordinate's performance improve, and the costs associated with the syndrome go away or, at least, decrease measurably.

In the second-best scenario, the subordinate's performance improves only marginally, but because the subordinate received an honest and open hearing from the boss, the relationship between the two becomes more productive. Boss and subordinate develop a better understanding of those job dimensions the subordinate can do well and those he struggles with. This improved understanding leads the boss and the subordinate to explore *together* how they can develop a better fit between the job and the subordinate's strengths and weaknesses. That improved fit can be achieved by significantly modifying the subordinate's existing job or by transferring the subordinate to another job within the company. It may even result in the subordinate's choosing to leave the company.

While that outcome is not as successful as the first one, it is still productive; a more honest relationship eases the strain on both the boss and the subordinate, and in turn on the subordinate's subordinates. If the subordinate moves to a new job within the organization that better suits him, he will likely become a stronger performer. His relocation may also open up a spot in his old job for a better performer. The key point is that, having been treated fairly, the subordinate is much more likely to accept the outcome of the process. Indeed, recent studies show that the perceived fairness of a process has a major impact on employees' reactions to its outcomes. (See "Fair Process: Managing in the Knowledge Economy," by W. Chan Kim and Renée Mauborgne, HBR July–August 1997.)

Such fairness is a benefit even in the cases where, despite the boss's best efforts, neither the subordinate's performance nor his relationship with his boss improves significantly. Sometimes this happens: The subordinate truly lacks the ability to meet the job requirements, he has no interest in making the effort to improve, and the boss and the subordinate have both professional and personal differences that are irreconcilable. In those cases, however, the intervention still yields indirect benefits because, even if termination follows, other employees within the company are less likely to feel expendable or betrayed when they see that the subordinate received fair treatment.

Prevention Is the Best Medicine

The set-up-to-fail syndrome is not an organizational fait accompli. It can be unwound. The first step is for the boss to become aware of its existence and acknowledge the possibility that he might be part of the problem. The second step requires that the boss initiate a clear, focused intervention. Such an intervention demands an open exchange between the boss and the subordinate based on the evidence of poor performance, its underlying causes, and their joint responsibilities—culminating in a joint decision on how to work toward eliminating the syndrome itself.

Reversing the syndrome requires managers to challenge their own assumptions. It also demands that they have the courage to look within themselves for causes and solutions before placing the burden of responsibility where it does not fully belong. Prevention of the syndrome, however, is clearly the best option.

In our current research, we examine prevention directly. Our results are still preliminary, but it appears that bosses who manage to consistently avoid the set-up-to-fail syndrome have several traits in common. They do not, interestingly, behave the same way with all subordinates. They are more involved with some subordinates than others—they even monitor some subordinates more than others. However, they do so without disempowering and discouraging subordinates.

How? One answer is that those managers begin by being actively involved with all their employees, gradually reducing their involvement based on improved performance. Early guidance is not threatening to subordinates, because it is not triggered by performance shortcomings; it is systematic and meant to help set the conditions for future success. Frequent contact in the beginning of the relationship gives the boss ample opportunity to communicate with subordinates about priorities, performance measures, time allocation, and even expectations of the type and frequency of communication. That kind of clarity goes a long way toward preventing the dynamic of the set-up-to-fail syndrome, which is so often fueled by unstated expectations and a lack of clarity about priorities.

For example, in the case of Steve and Jeff, Jeff could have made explicit very early on that he wanted Steve to set up a system that would analyze the root causes of quality control rejections systematically. He could have explained the benefits of establishing such a system during the initial stages of setting up the new production line, and he might have expressed his intention to be actively involved in the system's design and early operation. His future involvement might then have decreased in such a way that could have been jointly agreed on at that stage.

Another way managers appear to avoid the set-up-to-fail syndrome is by challenging their own assumptions and attitudes about employees on an ongoing basis. They work hard at resisting the temptation to categorize employees in simplistic ways. They also monitor their own reasoning. For example, when feeling frustrated about a subordinate's performance, they ask themselves, "What are the facts?" They examine whether they are expecting things from the employee that have not been articulated, and they try to be objective about how often and to what extent the employee has really failed. In other words, these bosses delve into their own assumptions and behavior before they initiate a full-blown intervention.

Finally, managers avoid the set-up-to-fail syndrome by creating an environment in which employees feel comfortable discussing their performance and their relationships with the boss. Such an environment is a function of several factors: the boss's openness, his comfort level with having his own opinions challenged, even his sense of humor. The net result is that the boss and the subordinate feel free to communicate frequently and to ask one another questions about their respective behaviors before problems mushroom or ossify.

The methods used to head off the set-up-to-fail syndrome do, admittedly, involve a great deal of emotional investment from bosses—just as interventions do. We believe, however, that this higher emotional involvement is the key to getting subordinates to work to their full potential. As with most things in life, you can only expect to get a lot back if you put a lot in. As a senior executive once said to us, "The respect you give is the respect you get." We concur. If you want—indeed, need—the people in your organization to devote their whole hearts and minds to their work, then you must, too.

Originally published in March–April 1998. Reprint 98209

Notes

1. The influence of expectations on performance has been observed in numerous experiments by Dov Eden and his colleagues. See Dov Eden, "Leadership and Expectations: Pygmalion Effects and Other Self-fulfilling Prophecies in Organizations," *Leadership Quarterly*, Winter 1992, vol. 3, no. 4, pp. 271–305.

2. Chris Argyris has written extensively on how and why people tend to behave unproductively in situations they see as threatening or embarrassing. See, for example, *Knowledge for Action: A Guide to Overcoming Barriers to Organizational Change* (San Francisco: Jossey-Bass, 1993).

Job Sculpting

The Art of Retaining Your Best People

by Timothy Butler and James Waldroop

BY ALL ACCOUNTS, *Mark was a star at the large West Coast bank where he had worked for three years. He had an MBA from a leading business school, and he had distinguished himself as an impressive "quant jock" and a skilled lending officer. The bank paid Mark well, and senior managers had every intention of promoting him. Little did they know he was seriously considering leaving the organization altogether.*

Hiring good people is tough, but as every senior executive knows, keeping them can be even tougher. Indeed, most executives can tell a story or two about a talented professional who joined their company to great fanfare, added enormous value for a couple of years, and then departed unexpectedly. Usually such exits are written off. "She got an offer she couldn't refuse," you hear, or, "No one stays with one company for very long these days."

Our research over the past 12 years strongly suggests that quite another dynamic is frequently at work. Many talented professionals leave their organizations because senior managers don't understand the psychology of work satisfaction; they assume that people who excel at their work are necessarily happy in their jobs. Sounds logical enough. But the fact is, strong skills don't always reflect or lead to job satisfaction. Many professionals, particularly the leagues of

20- and 30-somethings streaming out of today's MBA programs, are so well-educated and achievement-oriented that they could succeed in virtually any job. But will they stay?

The answer is, only if the job matches their *deeply embedded life interests*. These interests are not hobbies—opera, skiing, and so forth—nor are they topical enthusiasms, such as Chinese history, the stock market, or oceanography. Instead, deeply embedded life interests are long-held, emotionally driven passions, intricately entwined with personality and thus born of an indeterminate mix of nature and nurture. Deeply embedded life interests do not determine what people are good at—they drive what *kinds* of activities make them happy. At work, that happiness often translates into commitment. It keeps people engaged, and it keeps them from quitting.

In our research, we found only eight deeply embedded life interests for people drawn to business careers. (For a description of each one, see the sidebar "The Big Eight.") Life interests start showing themselves in childhood and remain relatively stable throughout our lives, even though they may manifest themselves in different ways at different times. For instance, a child with a nascent deeply embedded life interest in *creative production*—a love for inventing or starting things, or both—may be drawn to writing stories and plays. As a teenager, the life interest might express itself in a hobby of devising mechanical gadgets or an extracurricular pursuit of starting a high school sports or literary magazine. As an adult, the creative-production life interest might bubble up as a drive to be an entrepreneur or a design engineer. It might even show itself as a love for stories again—pushing the person toward a career in, say, producing movies.

Think of a deeply embedded life interest as a geothermal pool of superheated water. It will rise to the surface in one place as a hot spring and in another as a geyser. But beneath the surface—at the core of the individual—the pool is constantly bubbling. Deeply embedded life interests always seem to find expression, even if a person has to change jobs—or careers—for that to happen.

Idea in Brief

The Question

Hiring good people is tough but keeping them can be even tougher. The professionals streaming out of today's MBA programs are so well-educated and achievement-oriented that they could do well in virtually any job. But will they stay?

The Answer

According to career experts Timothy Butler and James Waldroop, only if their jobs fit their deeply embedded life interests—that is, their long-held, emotionally driven passions. Butler and Waldroop identify eight different life interests of people drawn to business careers and introduce the concept of job sculpting, the art of matching people to jobs that resonate with the activities that make them truly happy.

In Practice

Managers don't need special training to job sculpt, but they do need to listen more carefully when employees describe what they like and dislike about their jobs. Once managers and employees have discussed deeply embedded life interests—ideally, during employee performance reviews—they can work together to customize future work assignments. That may mean simply adding another assignment to existing responsibilities or it may require moving that employee to a new position altogether.

Job sculpting is the art of matching people to jobs that allow their deeply embedded life interests to be expressed. It is the art of forging a customized career path in order to increase the chance of retaining talented people. Make no mistake—job sculpting is challenging; it requires managers to play both detective and psychologist. The reason: Many people have only a dim awareness of their own deeply embedded life interests. They may have spent their lives fulfilling other people's expectations of them, or they may have followed the most common career advice: "Do what you're good at." For example, we know of a woman who, on the basis of her skill at chemistry in college, was urged to become a doctor. She complied and achieved great success as a neurologist, but at age 42 she finally quit to open a nursery school. She loved children, demonstrating a deeply embedded life interest in *counseling and mentoring*. And more important,

The Big Eight

WE HAVE FOUND THAT MOST PEOPLE IN BUSINESS are motivated by between one and three deeply embedded life interests—long-held, emotionally driven passions for certain kinds of activities. Deeply embedded life interests are not hobbies or enthusiasms; they are innate passions that are intricately entwined with personality. Life interests don't determine what we're good at but what kinds of work we love.

Our conclusions about the number and importance of deeply embedded life interests have grown out of more than a decade of research into the drivers of career satisfaction. In 1986, we began interviewing professionals from a wide range of industries and functions as well as asking them to take a battery of psychological tests in order to assess what factors contributed to work satisfaction. Over the next dozen years, our database had grown to 650 people.

The results of our research were striking: Scales on several of the tests we used clearly formed eight separate clusters. In other words, all business work could be broken down into eight types of core activities. By looking more closely at the content of the scales in each cluster and by cross-referencing this information to our interview data and counseling experience, we developed and tested a model of what we call "business core functions." These core functions represent the way deeply embedded life interests find expression in business. The following is a summary of each:

Application of Technology

Whether or not they are actually working as—or were trained to be—engineers, people with the life interest application of technology are intrigued by the inner workings of things. They are curious about finding better ways to use technology to solve business problems. We know a successful money manager who acts as his company's unofficial computer consultant because he loves the challenge of unlocking code. Indeed, he loves it more than his "day job"! People with the application-of-technology life interest often enjoy work that involves planning and analyzing production and operations systems and redesigning business processes.

It's often easy to recognize people with a strong application-of-technology life interest. They speak fondly of their college years when they majored in computer science or engineering. They read software magazines and manuals for fun. They comment excitedly when the company installs new hardware.

But sometimes the signs are more subtle. Application-of-technology people often approach business problems with a "let's take this apart and solve it" mindset. And when introduced to a new process at work, they like to get under the hood and fully understand how it works rather than just turn the key and drive it. In a snapshot, application-of-technology people are the ones who want to know how a clock works because the technology excites them—as does the possibility that it could be tinkered with and perhaps improved.

Quantitative Analysis

Some people aren't just good at running the numbers, they excel at it. They see it as the best, and sometimes the only, way to figure out business solutions. Similarly, they see mathematical work as fun when others consider it drudgery, such as performing a cash-flow analysis, forecasting the future performance of an investment instrument, or figuring out the best debt/equity structure for a business. They might also enjoy building computer models in order to determine optimal production scheduling and to perform accounting procedures.

Not all "quant jocks" are in jobs that reflect this deeply embedded life interest. In fact, many of these individuals find themselves in other kinds of work because they have been told that following their true passion will narrow their career prospects. Yet these people are not difficult to miss, because regardless of their assignment, they gravitate toward numbers. Consider the HR professional who analyzes his organization by looking at compensation levels and benefits and by studying the ratio of managers to employees. Similarly, a marketing manager who loves analyzing customer research data—versus the subjective findings of focus groups—is probably a person with quantitative analysis at her core.

Theory Development and Conceptual Thinking

For some people, nothing brings more enjoyment than thinking and talking about abstract ideas. Think of Mark, the West Coast banker who was frustrated in his position because he did not have the opportunity to ponder big-picture strategy. Like Mark, people with this deeply embedded life interest are drawn to theory—the why of strategy interests them much more than the how. People with this interest can be excited by building business models that explain competition within a given industry or by analyzing the competitive position of a business within a particular market. Our research also shows that people with this deeply embedded interest are often drawn to academic careers. Some end up there; many do not.

How can you identify the people with this interest? For starters, they're not only conversant in the language of theory, but they also genuinely enjoy talking about abstract concepts. Often, these are the people who like thinking about situations from the 30,000-foot level. Another clue: These individuals often subscribe to periodicals that have an academic bent.

Creative Production

Some people always enjoy the beginning of projects the most, when there are many unknowns and they can make something out of nothing. These individuals are frequently seen as imaginative, out-of-the-box thinkers. They seem most engaged when they are brainstorming or inventing unconventional solutions. Indeed, they seem to thrive on newness. The reason: Creative production is one of their dominant deeply embedded life interests—making something original, be it a product or a process.

Our research shows that many entrepreneurs, R&D scientists, and engineers have this life interest. Many of them have an interest in the arts, but just as many don't. An entrepreneur we know has virtually no passion for the arts; his quite successful businesses over the years have included manufacturing decidedly unsexy paper bags and sealing tape.

There are, of course, many places in the business world where people with this interest can find satisfying work—new product development, for example, or advertising. Many people with this interest gravitate toward creative industries such as entertainment. Yet others, like one investment analyst we know, repress this life interest because they feel that it is "too soft" for business. Creative production, they believe, is for their off-hours.

Fortunately for managers, most creative-production people are not terribly hard to recognize. They wear their life interest on their sleeves—sometimes literally, by virtue of their choice of unconventional clothing, but almost always by how excited they are when talking about the new elements of a business or product. Oftentimes, they show little interest in things that are already established, no matter how profitable or state-of-the-art.

Counseling and Mentoring

For some people, nothing is more enjoyable than teaching—in business, that usually translates into coaching or mentoring. These individuals are driven by the deeply embedded life interest of counseling and mentoring, allowing them to guide employees, peers, and even clients to better performance. People with a high interest in counseling and mentoring are also often drawn to organizations, such as museums, schools, and hospitals, that provide products or services they perceive to hold a high social value. People like to counsel and mentor for many reasons. Some derive satisfaction when other people succeed; others love the feeling of being needed. Regardless, these people are drawn to work where they can help others grow and improve. We know, for instance, of a brand manager at a consumer goods company who was primarily responsible for designing her product's marketing and distribution plans. Yet she eagerly made time every week to meet one-on-one with several subordinates in order to provide feedback on their performance and answer any questions they had about the company and their careers. When it came time for her performance review, the brand manager's boss didn't bother to evaluate this counseling-and-mentoring work, saying that it wasn't technically part of the brand manager's job. It was, however, her favorite part.

People with a counseling-and-mentoring interest will make themselves known if their jobs include the opportunity to do so. But many people in this category don't get that chance. (New MBAs, in particular, are not asked to coach other employees for several years out.) However, you can sometimes identify counseling-and-mentoring people by their hobbies and volunteer work. Many are drawn to hands-on community service, such as the Big Brother Organization or literacy programs. People with a high interest in counseling and mentoring can be recognized by the fact that when they talk about their previous work they often talk fondly about the people who worked under them and where they are now—like a parent would talk about his or her children.

Managing People and Relationships

Longing to counsel and mentor people is one thing; wanting to manage them is another thing entirely. Individuals with this deeply embedded life interest enjoy dealing with people on a day-to-day basis. They derive a lot of satisfaction from workplace relationships—but they focus much more on outcomes than do people in the counseling-and-mentoring category. In other words, they're less interested in seeing people grow than in working with and through them to accomplish the goals of the business, whether it be building a product or making a sale. That is why people with this life interest often find happiness in line management positions or in sales careers.

Take Tom, a 32-year-old Harvard MBA who joined an internet start-up in Silicon Valley—mainly because that was what all his classmates were doing. Tom had an undergraduate degree and work experience in engineering, and so his new company put him right to work in its technology division. Tom had no subordinates and no clients and mainly spent his days talking to other engineers and testing prototypes. It was the perfect job for someone with Tom's background, but not for someone with his life interest in managing people and relationships. After six months, he was miserable.

Tom was about to quit when the company announced it needed someone to help set up and run a new manufacturing plant in Texas. Tom pounced on the job—he would ultimately be leading a staff of 300 and negotiating frequently with suppliers. He got the job and still holds it today, five years later. His desire to motivate, organize, and direct people has been happily fulfilled.

Enterprise Control

Sarah, an attorney, is a person who has loved running things ever since she was a child. At age five, she set up her first lemonade stand and refused to let her older brother and sister help pour the juice, set prices, or collect money. (She did, however, let them flag down customers.) As a teenager, Sarah ran a summer camp in her backyard. And in college, she was the president of not one but three major groups, including the student government. People accuse her of being a control freak, and Sarah doesn't argue—she is happiest when she has ultimate decision-making authority. She feels great when she is in charge of making things happen.

Wanting too much control can be unhealthy, both for the people themselves and for their organizations, but some people are driven—in quite healthy ways—by a deeply embedded life interest in enterprise control. Whether or not they like managing people, these people find satisfaction in making the decisions that determine the direction taken by a work team, a business unit, a company division, or an entire organization. Sarah was not particularly happy as a lawyer—a career she pursued at the behest of an influential college instructor, and her mother, a lawyer herself. But she did eventually fulfill her life interest in enterprise control when, after coming back from maternity leave, she asked to run the company's New York office, with 600 attorneys, clerks, and other staff. It was, she says, "a match made in heaven."

Enterprise-control people are easy to spot in organizations. They seem happiest when running projects or teams; they enjoy "owning" a transaction such as a trade or a sale. These individuals also tend to ask for as much responsibility as possible in any work situation. Pure interest in enterprise control can be seen as an interest in deal making or in strategy—a person with this life interest wants to be the CEO, not the COO. Investment bankers, for example, don't run ongoing operations but often demonstrate a very strong interest in enterprise control.

Influence Through Language and Ideas

Some people love ideas for their own sake, but others love expressing them for the sheer enjoyment that comes from storytelling, negotiating, or persuading. Such are people with the deeply embedded life interest of influence through language and ideas. They feel most fulfilled when they are writing or speaking—or both. Just let them communicate.

People in this category sometimes feel drawn to careers in public relations or advertising, but they often find themselves elsewhere, because speaking and writing are largely considered skills, not careers. And yet for some, effective communication is more than just a skill—it's a passion. One way to identify these individuals in your organization is to notice who volunteers for writing assignments. One MBA student we counseled joined a large consulting firm where, for three years, she did the standard analytical work of studying industry dynamics and so forth. When she heard that a partner had to create a report for a new client "that liked to see things in writing," she quickly offered her services. Her report was so persuasive—and she had such a fun experience writing it—that she was soon writing for the company full-time. Had her deeply embedded interest in communication not been met in-house, she surely would have sought it elsewhere.

People with strong interests in influence through language and ideas love persuasion of all sorts, spoken and written, verbal and visual. They enjoy thinking about their audience (whether one person or millions) and the best way to address them. And they enjoy spending time on communications both outside and inside the company. One woman we know who is the head of strategic planning for an entertainment company says, "I spend at least 75% of my time thinking about how to sell our findings to the CEO and other members of the executive team." Clearly, the amount of mental energy this executive devotes to persuasion characterizes her as an influence-through-language-and-ideas person.

As we've noted, it is not uncommon for managers to sense that an employee has more than one deeply embedded life interest. That is possible. The pairs of life interests that are most commonly found together are listed below:

- **Enterprise control with managing people and relationships.** These individuals want to run a business on a day-to-day basis but are also challenged by—and enjoy—managing people.

- **Managing people and relationships with counseling and mentoring.** These are the ultimate people-oriented professionals. They have a strong preference for service-management roles, enjoying the frontline aspects of working in high customer-contact environments. They also tend to enjoy human resources management roles.

- **Quantitative analysis with managing people and relationships.** These individuals like finance and finance-related jobs, yet they also find a lot of pleasure managing people toward goals.

- **Enterprise control with influence through language and ideas.** This is the most common profile of people who enjoy sales. (An interest in managing people and relationships is also often high among satisfied salespeople.) This combination is also found extensively among general managers—especially those who are charismatic leaders.

- **Application of technology with managing people and relationships.** This is the engineer, computer scientist, or other technically-oriented individual who enjoys leading a team.

- **Creative production with enterprise control.** This is the most common combination among entrepreneurs. These people want to start things and dictate where projects will go. "Give me the ball and I'll score" is their mantra.

as it turned out, she was also driven by a life interest in *enterprise control*, the desire to be in charge of an organization's overall operations. It was a long time before she stopped remarking, "All those years wasted."

Other people don't know their own deeply embedded life interests because they have taken the path of least resistance: "Well, my dad was a lawyer." Or they've simply been unaware of many career choices at critical points in their lives. Most college seniors and new MBAs set sail on their careers knowing very little about all the possible islands in the sea. And finally, some people end up in the wrong jobs because they have chosen, for reasons good and bad, to follow the siren songs of financial reward or prestige. Regardless of the reason, the fact is that a good number of people, at least up until midlife, don't actually know what kind of work will make them happy. (For more on the importance of life interests, abilities, and values in job satisfaction, see the sidebar "It's a Matter of Degree.")

Let's return to Mark, the lending officer at a West Coast bank. Mark was raised in San Francisco; his mother and father were doctors who fully expected their son to become a successful professional. In high school, Mark received straight A's. He went on to attend Princeton, where he majored in economics. Soon after graduation, he began working at a prestigious management consulting firm, where he showed great skill at his assignments: building financial spreadsheets and interpreting pro formas. As expected, Mark

It's a Matter of Degree

OVER THE PAST SEVERAL DECADES, countless studies have been conducted to discover what makes people happy at work. The research almost always focuses on three variables: ability, values, and life interests. In this article, we argue that life interests are paramount—but what of the other two? Don't they matter? The answer is yes, but less so.

Ability—meaning the skills, experience, and knowledge a person brings to the job—can make an employee feel competent. That's important; after all, research has shown that a feeling of incompetence hinders creativity, not to mention productivity. But although competence can certainly help a person get hired, its effect is generally short lived. People who are good at their jobs aren't necessarily engaged by them.

In the context of career satisfaction, values refer to the rewards people seek. Some people value money, others want intellectual challenge, and still others desire prestige or a comfortable lifestyle. People with the same abilities and life interests may pursue different careers based on their values. Take three people who excel at and love quantitative analysis. One might pursue a career as a professor of finance for the intellectual challenge. Another might go straight to Wall Street to reap the financial rewards. And a third might pursue whatever job track leads to the CEO's office—driven by a desire for power and influence.

Like ability, values matter. In fact, people rarely take jobs that don't match their values. A person who hates to travel would not jump at an offer from a management consulting firm. Someone who values financial security won't chase a career as an independent contractor. But people can be drawn into going down career paths because they have the ability and like the rewards—even though they're not interested in the work. After a short period of success, they become disenchanted, lose interest, and either quit or just work less productively.

That's why we have concluded that life interests are the most important of the three variables of career satisfaction. You can be good at a job—indeed, you generally need to be—and you can like the rewards you receive from it. But only life interests will keep most people happy and fulfilled over the long term. And that's the key to retention.

left the consulting firm to attend a respected business school and then afterward joined the bank. It was located near his family, and because of its size and growth rate, he thought it would offer him good opportunities for advancement.

Mark, not surprisingly, excelled at every task the bank gave him. He was smart and knew no other way to approach work than to give it his all. But over time, Mark grew more and more unhappy. He was a person who loved running his mind over and through theoretical and strategic what-ifs. (After college, Mark had seriously considered a career in academia but had been dissuaded by his parents.) Indeed, one of Mark's deeply embedded life interests was *theory development and conceptual thinking*. He could certainly excel at the nitty-gritty number crunching and the customer service that his lending job entailed, but those activities did nothing for his heart and soul, not to mention for his commitment to the organization.

Fortunately for both Mark and the bank, he was able to identify what kind of work truly excited him before he quit. Consulting a career counselor, Mark came to see what kind of work interested him and how that differed from his current job responsibilities. Using this insight, he was able to identify a role in the bank's new market development area that would bring his daily tasks in line with his deeply embedded interests. Mark's work now consists of competitive analysis and strategy formulation. He is thriving, and the bank is reaping the benefit of his redoubled energy—and his loyalty.

Career Development: Standard Operating Procedure

As we've said, managers botch career development—and retention—because they mistakenly assume people are satisfied with jobs they excel at. But there are other reasons why career development goes wrong. The first is the way jobs usually get filled, and the second is the fact that career development so often gets handed off to the human resources department.

Most people get moved or promoted in their organizations according to a preset schedule—a new assignment every 18 months, say—or when another position in the company opens up. In either case, managers must scramble. If six employees are all scheduled to get new assignments on August 1, for example, a manager has to play mix and match, and usually does so based on abilities. Who is likely, the manager will ask herself, to do best in which jobs? Similarly, when a position opens up and needs to be filled right away, a manager must ask, "What skills does the job require? Who has them or seems most likely to develop them quickly?"

Sometimes people move up in an organization because they demand it. A talented employee might, for example, inform his manager that he wants to graduate to a new role because he's not growing anymore. The typical manager then considers the employee's skills and tries to find a place in the organization where they can be applied again, this time with a bit of "stretch."

Stretch assignments, however, often do little to address deeply embedded life interests. A research assistant at an investment management firm who performs well can stretch her skills into a credit analyst role, and after continued success there, she can move into the position of fixed-income portfolio manager. But what if her deeper interests are in managing others? Or how about the "spot news" reporter who is "stretched" into management when her real passion (discovered, perhaps, through a few years of misadventure as a manager) lies in investigative reporting?

Skills can be stretched in many directions, but if they are not going in a direction that is congruent with deeply embedded life interests, then employees are at risk of becoming dissatisfied and uncommitted. In such situations, employees usually attribute their unhappiness to their managers or to their organizations. They'll decide their organization has the wrong culture, for example. That kind of thinking often leads to a "migration cure" of leaving one organization for another, only to find similar dissatisfaction because the root of the career malaise has not been identified and addressed. One individual we consulted, a manager in the high-tech industry, went through three companies before realizing it wasn't the company he needed to change but his work. He had never wanted to be a manager but had agreed to a promotion because it offered more money and prestige. All he really wanted to do was design intricate machinery and mechanisms; he wanted to be an engineer again.

That story brings us to the second reason career development is handled poorly. The engineer was originally promoted to manager at the suggestion of the human resources department. Generally speaking, we have found that when career development is handed off to HR, problems arise. Many HR managers try to tackle career development using standardized tests such as the Myers-Briggs Type Indicator. There is nothing wrong with the Myers-Briggs and tests like it. In fact, they are excellent when used to help teams understand their own working dynamics. But personality type should not be the foundation of career development. Some HR managers do use the Strong Interest Inventory to get at life interests, which is better, but it suffers from being too general. The Strong helps people who want to know if they should be a Marine Corps sergeant or a ballet dancer, but it does little for people who say, "I know I want to work in business. Exactly what type of job is best for me?"

The bigger problem with allowing HR to handle career development is that it cuts the manager out of the process. Career development in general, and job sculpting in particular, requires an ongoing dialogue between an employee and his boss; it should not be shunted to another department, however good it may be. HR adds its value in training and supporting managers as career developers.

The Techniques of Job Sculpting

Job sculpting, then, begins when managers identify each employee's deeply embedded life interests. Sometimes an employee's life interest is glaringly obvious—she is excited doing one kind of work and dismal doing another. But much more often, a manager has to probe and observe.

Some managers worry that job sculpting requires them to play psychologist. They shouldn't worry. If they're good managers, they already play the role of psychologist intuitively. Managers *should* have a strong interest in the motivational psychology of their employees. In fact, they should openly express their willingness to help sculpt their employees' careers and to make the extra effort required to hold onto talented people.

Job sculpting, incidentally, can also be marketed externally to attract new hires. We have an unusual vantage point: We've seen close to a thousand new business professionals recruited and hired every year for the last 20 years. Without a doubt, the single most important thing on the minds of new MBAs is—not money!—but whether a position will move their long-term careers in a chosen direction. In fact, during a recent recruiting season, one employer— a Wall Street firm—gained a significant advantage over its competitors by emphasizing its commitment to career development. In both presentations and individual discussions, executives from the firm described its interest in and commitment to helping its professionals think about and manage their careers—a fact that many students cited as key to their choosing that firm.

If managers promise to job sculpt, of course they have to deliver. But how? Each change in assignment provides an opportunity to do some sculpting. For instance, a salesperson with an interest in *quantitative analysis* might be given new duties working with the marketing product manager and market research analysts—while remaining in sales. Or an engineer with an interest in *influence through language and ideas* might be given the task of helping the marketing communications people design sales support materials or user manuals— again, while retaining her primary role as an engineer.

But we have found that such intermittent patching attempts at job sculpting are not nearly as effective as bringing the process directly into the regular performance review. An effective performance review dedicates time to discussing past performance and plans for the future. In making job sculpting part of those conversations, it becomes systematized, and in becoming systematized, the chances of someone's career "falling through the cracks" are minimized.

Do managers need special training to job sculpt? No, but they do need to start listening more carefully when employees describe what they like and dislike about their jobs. Consider the case of a pharmaceutical company executive who managed 30 salespeople. In a performance review, one of her people offhandedly mentioned that her favorite part of the past year had been helping their division find new office space and negotiating for its lease. "That was a blast. I loved it," she told her boss. In the past, the executive would have paid the comment little heed. After all, what did it have to do with the woman's performance in sales? But listening with the ears of a job sculptor, the executive probed further, asking, "What made the search for new office space fun for you?" and "How was that different from what you do day-to-day?" The conversation revealed that the saleswoman was actually very dissatisfied and bored with her current position and was considering leaving. In fact, the saleswoman yearned for work that met her deeply embedded life interests, which had to do with *influence through language and ideas* and *creative production*. Her sales job encompassed the former, but it was only when she had the chance to think about the location, design, and layout of the new office that her creativity could be fully expressed. The manager helped the woman move to a position at company headquarters, where her primary responsibility was to design marketing and advertising materials.

Along with listening carefully and asking probing questions during the performance review, managers can ask employees to play an active role in job sculpting—before the meeting starts. In most corporate settings, the employee's preparation for a performance review includes a written assessment of accomplishments, goals for the upcoming review period, skill areas in need of development, and plans for accomplishing both goals and growth. During the review, this assessment is then compared to the supervisor's assessment.

But imagine what would happen if employees were also expected to write up their personal views of career satisfaction. Imagine if they were to prepare a few paragraphs on what kind of work they love or if they described their favorite activities on the job. Because so many people are unaware of their deeply embedded life interests—not to mention unaccustomed to discussing them with their managers—such exercises might not come easily at first. Yet they would be an excellent starting point for a discussion, ultimately allowing employees to speak more clearly about what they want from work, both in the short and long term. And that information would make even the best job-sculpting managers more effective.

Once managers and employees have discussed deeply embedded life interests, it's time to customize the next work assignment accordingly. In cases where the employee requires only a small change in his activities, that might just mean adding a new responsibility. For example, an engineer who has a deeply embedded life interest in *counseling and mentoring* might be asked to plan and manage the orientation of new hires. Or a logistics planner with a deeply embedded life interest in *influence through language and ideas* could be given the task of working on recruitment at college campuses. The goals here would be to give some immediate gratification through an immediate and real change in the job and to begin the process of moving the individual to a role that more fully satisfies him.

Sometimes, however, job sculpting calls for more substantial changes. Mark, the dissatisfied bank lending officer is one example. Another is Carolyn, who was a star industry analyst at a leading Wall Street firm. Carolyn was so talented at designing and using sophisticated new quantitative approaches to picking stocks that at one point the head of the entire division remarked, "Carolyn has brought our business into the twenty-first century." That same year, she was ranked as the second most valuable person within the entire group— out of almost a hundred very talented finance professionals. For the past several years, senior managers had sought to ensure Carolyn's loyalty to the organization by awarding her generous raises and bonuses, making her one of their highest paid people.

But Carolyn had one foot out the door. When she received a huge raise (even by the standards of this firm and her own compensation history), she was actually angry, commenting to a friend, "That's typical of this company; it thinks that it can solve every problem by throwing money at it." Although she loved analysis and mathematics, she had a strong desire to have a greater impact on the decision-making and direction of the research group. She had definite opinions regarding what kind of people they should be hiring, how the group should be organized and the work assigned and how the group could most effectively work with other departments—in other words, she had deeply embedded life interests in *enterprise control* and *managing people and relationships*.

A performance review gave Carolyn a chance to express her dreams and frustrations to her boss. Together they arrived at a "player-coach" role for Carolyn as coordinator of research. She was still an analyst, but she also had taken on the responsibilities of guiding and directing several teams, making decisions about hiring and promotions, and helping set strategic direction. A year later, all parties agreed that the research group had never been more productive.

Job sculpting allowed Carolyn's firm to keep some of her extraordinary skills as an analyst while satisfying her desire to manage. But oftentimes job sculpting involves more sacrifice on the part of the organization. Remember that when Mark moved to his new job in business development, the bank lost a talented lending officer. Sometimes job sculpting requires short-term pain for long-term gain, although we would argue that in Mark's case—and in many others like it—they would have lost him soon enough anyway.

And one final caveat emptor. When job sculpting requires taking away parts of a job an employee dislikes, it also means finding someone new to take them on. If staffing levels are sufficient, that won't be a problem—an uninteresting part of one person's job may be perfect for someone else. At other times, however, there won't be a knight in shining armor to take on the "discarded" work. And at still other times, a manager may recognize that there is simply no way to accomplish the job sculpting the employee wants or even needs. (For instance, an engineering firm may not have activities to satisfy a person with a life interest in *influence through language and ideas*.) In such a case, a manager may have to make the hard choice to counsel a talented employee to leave the company.

Even with its challenges, job sculpting is worth the effort. In the knowledge economy, a company's most important asset is the energy and loyalty of its people—the intellectual capital that, unlike machines and factories, can quit and go to work for your competition. And yet, many managers regularly undermine that commitment by allowing talented people to stay in jobs they're doing well at but aren't fundamentally interested in. That just doesn't make sense. To turbocharge retention, you must first know the hearts and minds of your employees and then undertake the tough and rewarding task of sculpting careers that bring joy to both.

Originally published in September–October 1999. Reprint 99502

Performance Management Shouldn't Kill Collaboration

by Heidi K. Gardner and Ivan Matviak

LEADERS AT TECHCO, a fast-growing maker of marketing analytics software (a real firm we've disguised for this article), faced a puzzling problem: Though the sales and installation teams were hitting all their targets, many new customers were seriously dissatisfied. Digging in, the executives discovered that while each department was measuring its teams' performance at their respective tasks, no one had any incentive to ensure that all the pieces fit together—that the software was customized to generate accurate analytics for each customer's complex, nuanced requirements and went live on time. As a result, customers were complaining loudly.

TechCo urgently needed to improve cross-silo collaboration—a solution that would also offer it benefits well beyond happier customers. Cross-silo collaboration, as we have seen in our research and advisory work with hundreds of companies over the past decade, can help organizations cope with a volatile competitive environment, innovate faster, and grow revenues. In one global bank we studied, for example, improved collaboration among specialists in branches (mortgage officers, investment advisers, data analysts, tellers) increased customer service scores by 8% and the branches' financial performance by 17%. When one consulting firm improved collaboration among its partners, its annual revenues rose 34%. Collaboration also boosts retention: Our studies show that new hires who get pulled onto others' projects and have people jump in to help on theirs are at least 65% more likely than more-isolated peers to stay long enough at the company to become productive and profitable.

The main problem at TechCo—a siloed approach to target setting—is one of the top barriers to collaboration, according to our research involving more than 8,000 senior managers in sectors ranging from biotech and banking to automotive, consumer products, energy, and law. When companies cascade their broad corporate goals down through the ranks, they often use scorecards that encourage managers and employees to take an overly narrow, short-term view of performance. In scrambling to hit their numbers, people lose sight of larger goals and jockey for resources or credit. That competitive dynamic contributes to stress and burnout.

There's a much better way to set goals and their related metrics. In this article we'll describe how and outline specific actions companies can take to shift their overall performance management systems toward boosting the collaboration they need.

Common Mistakes That Undermine Collaboration

In organizations around the globe, we have found that performance management systems are often flawed in some or all of five ways.

Key performance indicators aren't focused on customer satisfaction

This was a crucial omission at TechCo. The company's sales reps were so fixated on getting deals signed to hit their individual revenue targets that they didn't accurately or completely document clients' needs. Often the reps glossed over the more-complex requirements and capability gaps to get the orders closed. TechCo's engineers then started working on detailed implementation plans, but the lack of clarity in the sales process caused customer confusion about the promised scope of work and functionality. What's more, because the

Idea in Brief

The Ambition

Leaders set broad corporate goals and want all functions to collaborate to achieve them.

The Problem

Performance management systems often use scorecards that encourage managers and employees to take an overly narrow, short-term view of performance that undermines collaboration. In scrambling to hit their numbers, people lose sight of larger goals and jockey for resources or credit.

The Solution

Institute a four-part performance scorecard that establishes shared goals on strategic targets while still holding employees accountable for delivering individual results. Each component should be weighted according to its importance in helping the company reach its strategic aims.

performance of the engineers was measured by installation time, they were motivated to cut corners. Then, after the installation went live, TechCo's client service teams were left to clean up the mess.

That isn't unusual. Companies typically set broad, overarching, collaboration-dependent goals, like revenue growth or faster innovation, and then create myriad targets for functions and divisions and units that are based on the conventional wisdom that people should be held accountable only for outcomes they directly control. But these narrow goals cause employees to optimize their own results and not consider their actions' impact on other parts of the business. Systems that use them can pit groups against one another, motivate people to hoard staff or knowledge, create a culture of blame, weaken employee engagement, and leave customers unhappy and angry.

Incentives for collaboration are piecemeal

At one consulting firm the CEO set aside $80,000 for quarterly rewards to team leaders who worked across service lines. After three quarters, less than 10% of the pot had been given away, and he called us in for advice. The firm's mistake, we told him, was a common one: Rewards for collaboration are added on to the incentive system as an afterthought instead of being integrated into it. Because they aren't tied directly to the achievement of major strategic objectives, employees consider them to be peripheral and view them cynically. "It's total BS," a manager at the firm confided to us. "The whole system is designed to make us focus on hitting our individual numbers, and then a couple times a year they come out pretending that collaboration is really important."

Rewards are tied to input rather than output

At one global consumer-products company, brand managers were awarded bonuses for adding information about their successful marketing campaigns to a knowledge management database. When the results were unimpressive, the SVP of marketing turned to us for help. "We got dozens of posts," she told us, "but very few of them had enough detail, analysis, or insights to help others replicate the success." We see this kind of scenario all the time. Rather than motivating people to achieve a strategic goal like improving the effectiveness of a firm's marketing, input-driven metrics encourage them to game the system. People take shortcuts to secure the bonus and don't invest the time needed to genuinely collaborate.

Rewards for visionary goals are lumped together with those for short-term objectives

Many companies with big long-term ambitions—such as achieving a carbon-neutral footprint or using AI to create more-dynamic and resilient supply chains—struggle to get employees to take action on them. Their mistake is not separating rewards for them from those for more-tangible, shorter-term, easily quantified objectives.

Psychologists studying delayed gratification have long documented people's tendency to trade off large future rewards for near-term gains. People enjoy the frequent dopamine boosts they get from small wins. Moreover, managers tend to give out bonuses and raises for the more-tangible achievements. When we recently analyzed multiple years of compensation practices at several professional service firms, for example, we found that they all emphasized the importance of activities with longer-term payoffs, such as developing significant new thought-leadership areas. But while the firms collected data on the initiatives and included them in partners' scorecards, our analyses showed that they had zero effect on the partners' compensation. The firms didn't assign any weighting to those long-term outcomes, so the leaders ended up basing bonus decisions only on concrete wins that had near-term impact.

Cross-selling is confused with collaboration

Many companies award bonuses for persuading existing customers to buy additional products or services. The problem is that this encourages employees to look at customers in a purely transactional way (as opportunities to sell more widgets) rather than seek to understand their complex problems and then collaborate with colleagues to provide valuable holistic solutions.

Companies can avoid these five flawed approaches by adopting a four-part performance scorecard that establishes shared goals to encourage collaboration on strategic targets while still holding employees accountable for delivering individual results. Each component should be weighted according to its importance in helping the company reach its strategic aims, but we recommend over-weighting the collective goals to counteract people's natural tendency to pay more attention to their individual metrics. To keep employees focused on what the organization truly values, each part should contain no more than a few goals.

To see how this works in practice, consider the scorecards that were created for functional executives, regional managers, and individual employees in TechCo's sales, implementation, and client service departments in the United States. (Similar scorecards were implemented internationally.)

Component One: Ambitious Cross-Silo Goals

Broad shared goals that focus on big challenges and can be achieved within a year help break down organizational silos and get teams working together across functions. Such challenges might involve things like halving the time to market for new products or doubling

The scorecard: component one

To focus everyone on increasing new customers' satisfaction, all employees in the three functions are given similar goals.

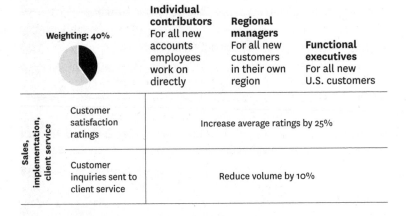

Weighting: 40%		**Individual contributors** For all new accounts employees work on directly	**Regional managers** For all new customers in their own region	**Functional executives** For all new U.S. customers
Sales, implementation, client service	Customer satisfaction ratings	Increase average ratings by 25%		
	Customer inquiries sent to client service	Reduce volume by 10%		

revenue from certain customers. When identifying them, it's often easiest to start with the customer, by asking what overall experience and result the customer wants. Another approach is to focus on a strategic outcome that will strengthen your company—such as diversifying its supply chain. After you determine which groups can influence the desired outcome, you should embed it as a goal in the scorecards for all of them.

At TechCo the leaders set a bold goal of increasing new-customer satisfaction ratings by 25% in 12 months. This was the primary component-one goal given to every executive, regional manager, and employee in the sales, implementation, and client service functions, and component one was the most heavily weighted (representing 40% of employees' bonuses) in the scorecards. To measure progress on it, the company not only surveyed customers twice a year but also tracked the volume of inquiries the client service team got—a leading indicator of quality—with an eye toward reducing them by 10%. The cross-silo goals motivated people in all three functions to look beyond their responsibilities and work together to find ways to improve the overall customer experience.

Employees at all levels were measured on the satisfaction of the customers they were responsible for: individuals, for the specific accounts they handled; regional department managers, for all clients in their own region; and U.S. functional executives, for all U.S. customers. (Goals in other parts of the scorecard motivated people to collaborate across geographies with counterparts in their own departments.)

The customer surveys highlighted the disconnect between the clients' business requirements and what TechCo actually delivered, which as we've noted began when the salespeople left the details of the contracts to be sorted out later. To address that particular problem, the leaders of sales and implementation jointly redesigned the order forms to document client requirements more granularly. Then they set up a formal client sign-off process to ensure that everyone was clear about the deliverables. Next the leaders of the implementation and client service teams agreed to get their people involved earlier in the sales process to uncover and resolve any potential gaps or misunderstanding about capabilities that might damage a client's perceptions of the final product.

Component Two: Team Goals

Organizations need to break down barriers to collaboration not only across functions but also *within* them. Team members must share best practices and ideas, learn from one another, and work together to achieve collective targets. To encourage this, firms should measure team-level results and hold people accountable for raising the performance of their whole working group, whether it's a functional department, a key account team, or a product development team.

Take the implementation teams at TechCo. Previously, they had no department-level goals that would focus people on improving the quality and speed of all initial customer set-ups. Instead, each team was assessed on only its own projects. There was little motivation to exchange information and tips, which meant that work was frequently delayed while people reinvented the wheel.

The scorecard: component two

To promote collaboration across geographic teams, individual contributors are held accountable for hitting their function's regional target, and regional managers and functional executives for hitting national and global goals, respectively.

Weighting: 30%	Individual contributors For entire region	Regional managers For all five U.S. regions combined	Functional executives Across the company worldwide
Sales			
Sales	$5 million	$25 million	$50 million
Pipeline of prospective sales	$20 million	$100 million	$200 million
Employee engagement score (out of 5)	—	3.5 or more	3.5 or more
Implementation			
Percentage of functionality at "go live"	100%	100%	100%
Percentage of projects done on time	95%	95%	95%
Employee engagement score (out of 5)	—	3.5 or more	3.5 or more
Client service			
Inquiry resolution (average)	Less than 5 hours	Less than 5 hours	Less than 5 hours
Monthly inquiry resolution (average)	95%	95%	95%
Employee engagement score (out of 5)	—	3.5 or more	3.5 or more

In the new scorecards the performance of each individual on an implementation team was measured by the success of all projects within the region. Meanwhile, to keep regional managers focused on sharing best practices and collaborating with their peers in other regions, they were evaluated on the success of implementations across the entire country. In addition, because collaboration hinges on people's willingness to be creative and take some risks—a mindset that's hard to promote in burned-out, disaffected employees—the managers had to meet metrics tied to engagement. The intrateam component was given a 30% weighting, the second highest.

The collective goals promoted a sense of shared purpose among the teams. "Engineers across teams started helping each other more," the head of implementation told us. "They set up a community on our intranet so that they could exchange ideas about how to solve specific problems and started standardizing best practices that made the process faster. During Covid, when we had lots of staff shortages, they set up an SOS system so that they could quickly swap resources between customers. In the old system they would have hoarded their people for their own projects."

In a similar manner, the scorecards of U.S. functional executives included a metric for worldwide outcomes, motivating them to collaborate with their counterparts who led functions in other countries, and a metric for employee engagement.

Component Three: Individual Goals

Well-designed individual targets not only promote personal accountability but also directly connect to team and organization-wide objectives. They help each person understand how his or her specific actions contribute to higher-level success.

Let's look at TechCo's client service teams. Under the old system, individual help specialists had been evaluated just on how long it took them to resolve each client inquiry and how many inquiries each person completed in a day. Those metrics drove high productivity but not customer satisfaction. Service specialists had no incentive to address underlying issues such as poor data quality, which stemmed from the failure to modify the software for each customer's needs. The new system, in contrast, motivated the client service professionals—who had real-time, sometimes visceral perspectives on customers' experiences—to be more proactive.

The scorecard: component three

Employees are individually accountable for achieving their part of shared goals. That includes helping tackle common customer problems by participating in cross-functional task forces. (Note: Under individual contributors, only goals for data-quality task force members are shown.)

Weighting: 15%

		Individual contributors For assigned accounts	Regional managers For region overseen	Functional executives For entire U.S.
Sales	Sales	$1 million	$5 million	$20 million
	Pipeline of prospective sales	$4 million	$20 million	$80 million
	Task force	Propose solutions to reduce inquiries on two data-quality issues	Lead an AI automation task force	Sponsor a task force on data quality
	Employee engagement score (out of 5)	—	3.5 or more	3.5 or more
Implementation	Percentage of functionality at "go live"	100%	100%	100%
	Percentage of projects done on time	95%	95%	95%
	Employee engagement score (out of 5)	—	3.5 or more	3.5 or more
	Task force	Propose solutions to reduce inquiries on two data-quality issues	Lead a task force on report timeliness	Sponsor a task force on AI automation
Client service	Inquiry resolution (average)	Less than 5 hours	Less than 5 hours	Less than 5 hours
	Monthly inquiry resolution (average)	95%	95%	95%
	Employee engagement score (out of 5)	—	3.5 or more	3.5 or more
	Task force	Propose solutions to reduce inquiries on two data-quality issues	Lead a task force on data-quality issues	Sponsor a task force on report timeliness

The company began by creating three task forces, drawing members from all three departments, to solve common problems that led to customer inquiries. One task force focused on improving data quality, another on increasing on-time implementation, and the third on using artificial intelligence to enhance operations. Each task force was led by a regional manager and sponsored by a functional executive from a different department, who coached the regional manager and helped the task force get resources. The scorecards of the individual members included a goal of proposing solutions to the problem each group was addressing. (The regional managers leading the task forces were accountable for implementing those solutions and were asked to reduce the number of inquiries related to data quality by 20%, increase on-time implementation by 30%, and introduce AI into three processes, respectively.)

The third part of the client service professionals' scorecards also included individual goals for their "day job" of handling inquiries from customers they were assigned to. (Giving everyone in a team personal targets related to the team goals is important to discourage free-riding and stop members from worrying that others won't do their share.) Altogether the component-three goals were weighted 15%. That was large enough to instill a strong sense of personal accountability while still ensuring collaboration on the higher-level goals.

Component Four: Long-Range Programs

The first three parts of the scorecard lay out goals that can be largely achieved during a single annual performance cycle. To focus employees on longer-term, multidisciplinary initiatives, a fourth component is needed. Goals here might include developing white papers that showcase a company's cutting-edge ideas; sizable pro bono projects that draw on an array of capabilities and allow employees to stretch their skills; and significantly upping diversity at all levels of the company. Measuring progress on such long-term goals allows companies to factor work on them into compensation and promotion decisions. Moreover, the trusting interpersonal

The scorecard: component four

Employees are also expected to invest time in projects that take longer than a year—such as an initiative to enter a new market segment. Here individual contributors lead the research process, and a regional manager and a functional executive are tasked with applying the findings with prospective customers.

Weighting: 15%

Sales, implementation, client service		Selected individuals	Selected regional manager	One functional executive
	Roundtable	Organize three roundtables of prospective customers		
	Roundtable surveys	Score 90% on surveys about roundtable value		
	Codevelopment partners		Get three customers in new market to codevelop new capabilities	
	Pilot			Pilot the beta product with two customers by year-end

relationships the people who take part in these activities develop will strengthen future collaboration.

At TechCo leaders set a longer-term goal of entering a completely new customer segment within three years. The CEO tasked the three departments with creating a compelling proposition for this segment that they could effectively sell, implement, and service. The three function heads jointly selected a team of regional managers and individual contributors from the three departments to focus on that objective, choosing people who not only had diverse expertise but also would benefit from working on more-complex projects with other departments. The team members' scorecards included targets that could be achieved in the first year: completing a series of roundtable discussions with senior executives at firms that were prospective customers to glean an understanding of their unaddressed needs, the market segment's competitive dynamics, buying patterns, and so on.

To ensure that the task force didn't just go through the motions, its members were given targets related to the seniority of the roundtable participants (who needed to have deep knowledge of the market segment) and for those participants' post-event feedback about the roundtables' value. To make sure regional managers and functional executives assigned to the project followed through on what the teams learned during the discussions, the managers' targets included securing three prospective customers to help develop the new product, and the executives' targets included piloting the beta product with at least two customers. Everyone's goals in this section were given a 15% weighting.

Revamp Supporting Processes

To test the effect of differing performance management systems on collaboration, one Big Four accounting firm ran two pilots. In one region it added collective goals to partners' key performance indicators. That led to an 8% increase in sales, in part because the firm cross-sold work to clients that had previously bought just one type of service. In another region the collective goals were paired with changes in related processes, such as a shift from annual to monthly performance discussions and training for leaders on how to coach their reports. The second region's results were far greater: Revenue climbed 30%, employee engagement scores hit a new high, and client satisfaction rose dramatically.

As these results show, companies must ensure they have the right processes to support new goals and incentives. Implementing the following practices will help.

Separate discussions about development and compensation

If you meet with your boss to discuss your annual bonus and your development goals for next year, which part of the conversation do you really focus on? For most people it's the bonus. So discussions of compensation should only address individuals' success in achieving the goals in their scorecards. Conversations about employees' professional development—their strengths and areas to improve, the training and growth experiences they need—should take place in a separate meeting. Although scholars such as Peter Cappelli have long advocated for this bifurcated approach (see "The Performance Management Revolution," HBR, October 2016), many companies have yet to adopt it. Giving equal weight to financial outcomes and development underscores the importance of learning and growth. And a learning culture enhances collaboration by promoting employees' curiosity and interest in others' work, as research by Harvard Business School's Francesca Gino and others has shown.

Don't assign numerical ratings

People would rather hear "You're meeting, not exceeding, expectations" than "You're a 3 on a 5-point scale." In our work across industries, everyone from top executives to recent graduates tells us that being reduced to a number is demoralizing. Even worse is the practice of forced-curve benchmarking against peers. Studies have shown that it destroys collaboration because it's a zero-sum game. You can't expect coworkers who are pitted against one another to work together effectively. Rather than comparing people with their peers, managers should focus monthly and year-end development discussions on employees' performance trajectories: Are people growing, working effectively across silos, and increasing their impact not just individually but also as contributors to the broader organization?

Align the frequency of feedback with work milestones

Most companies have moved away from a strictly annual feedback process and have either implemented shorter cycles, perhaps providing formal feedback quarterly, or instructed managers to deliver it on an ongoing basis. A better approach is to link the cadence of feedback to milestones in work. For example, since a call center's workers have extremely short-term targets, such as for daily call quality, their managers should sit down with them for weekly reviews. With long-term goals, you can schedule feedback meetings at strategic interim milestones. At TechCo, for instance, where the long-term ambition was to enter a new customer segment, feedback discussions for individuals could be linked to the completion of half the prospective-customer roundtables.

Use creative rewards

No matter how successful people are, they crave recognition for their good work, and that doesn't always mean financial rewards. Consider the way the NASA@Work program encourages innovators across the government to generate breakthroughs and solve important problems. Winners are rewarded not with money but with incentives like a personalized astronaut autograph, a visit to the employee's department by NASA top brass, or an external shout-out on NASA's Twitter account. Organizations can also take this approach when recognizing team outcomes. The more leaders can embed symbolic rewards for great collaboration, the more their systems will foster a collaborative culture.

Discuss how performance was delivered

Two people can produce the same result in very different ways: One might be constructive and collaborative, and the other "me-first" and sharp-elbowed. The second person may hit his or her targets, but the collateral damage can be real. How often have you been in an organization where you asked, "How can a person like that get ahead?" Frequently, it's because the organization values only the *what* and not the *how*. You need room in your compensation model for manager discretion to reward people who live up to the organization's values and to penalize people who don't. Conversations with the latter aren't easy, so make sure the values are well understood and managers are trained to deliver tough messages.

TechCo's leaders realized they needed to do more than just change the performance scorecards. They trained managers how to give more-effective, timely feedback and provided tools such as pulse surveys that helped department leaders stay abreast of team sentiment. They also eliminated forced rankings and numerical ratings—a move that 72% of respondents in a company survey cited as a major signal of leadership's new focus on a collaborative culture. Employee engagement scores rose dramatically, people reported that the performance management process seemed to be more fair, and customer satisfaction scores reached an all-time high.

———————

A well-designed performance management system, which aligns people across silos to achieve shared outcomes, is critical to increasing collaboration. When people start collaborating, the benefits for both business growth and employee engagement are dramatic.

Originally published in September–October 2022. Reprint R2205J

The Happy Tracked Employee

by Ben Waber

DISCUSSIONS ABOUT DATA PRIVACY TEND TO FOCUS on the consumer-seller dynamic. What personal information do companies have a right to collect, and how should they be expected to use and care for it? But another dynamic, between employer and worker, raises even thornier questions.

For years people analytics—the science of using data to manage employees—drew on details about age, gender, and tenure and ratings from performance reviews for insights. But that paltry harvest limited its usefulness.

More recently, sensor technology and real-time data collection have produced bumper crops of employee information for companies. Now managers can access second-by-second feedback on what a worker is doing and, to some extent, what a worker is feeling. Data from emails, chats, and calendar systems can be analyzed alongside traditional HR data. Sensors can gather incredibly granular data on workers' habits—everything from who speaks with whom, how much people interrupt one another, where they spend time, and even their stress levels. And as ID badges and office furniture join the internet of things, the information that companies have on their workers will expand by orders of magnitude. HR departments now have the potential to know nearly everything about employees.

Already, the new measurement tools have had an immensely positive impact—when deployed correctly and ethically. Companies have used data from wearable sensors and digital communication to quantify and reduce gender bias at work, increase alertness and reduce fatigue, significantly lift performance, and lower attrition, in industries from railways to finance to quick service restaurants. And we are just beginning to tap the potential of these new technologies.

For workers, though, the value of all this data gathering isn't as clear. Advanced people analytics may even hinder employees' ability to freely manage their time and experiment. The numbers might suggest, for instance, that a new way of working isn't productive, even though it could eventually lead to long-term company gains. Worse still, analytical tools open up the risk of abuse through Tayloristic overmonitoring.

Just because you *can* measure something doesn't mean you should. Workers' advocates worry that data-based surveillance gives employers unreasonable power over employees, and they aren't sure companies can be trusted not to lose or abuse sensitive personal information.

After all, companies' systems are frequently breached. And it's not a long leap from monitoring employees' stress to using health care data to predict medical conditions and take preemptive action. Data also gives a false sense of validity. That is, it can make certain conclusions seem true (employee X is not productive because he generates 10% less output) even if there are legitimate alternative points of view (employee X is productive in a different way—by, say, reducing errors or training others).

Given this new reality, managers now face challenging questions: Should they use analytical tools that examine employees' worktime habits to assess their performance? What data should firms have access to? Should they share their analyses with employees? Should they look at individual data? What about using data to determine the risk that an employee will develop a mental illness? Companies, lawmakers, and regulators are already starting to grapple with rules for the use of monitoring tools in the workplace.

Idea in Brief

The Opportunity

Using advanced technologies, organizations can now collect and track a wide range of employee information, from online communications to work habits—and even to their stress levels. Applying people analytics to this data can offer managers valuable insights and help them assess and improve their employees' performance.

The Problem

With such opportunity, though, comes challenges. Organizational leaders and managers must now navigate questions of whether they

should use these tools to assess performance, how transparent they should be, and how to do so ethically.

The Solution

Employee buy-in is essential to a successful people analytics program. When rolling out a new program, managers must allow employees to opt in, communicate clearly about the promise of the proposed program and be willing to answer questions, aggregate the data to ensure anonymity, and look beyond the numbers to ensure they're measuring the right things.

In the meantime, managers need guidance on how to run effective and ethical people analytics programs that will avoid an employee backlash or a heavy-handed legislative response. Through my work at MIT with Sandy Pentland and in designing products and services for my own analytics company, I have identified several scientifically backed ground rules for the use of monitoring technology. I've seen these techniques effectively mitigate potential issues, and I've seen serious problems arise when they weren't used.

In general, successful rollouts of people analytics technologies take four to six weeks. While faster implementation may be possible in some organizations, it's important to do it right. That will show employees that management is being thoughtful about thorny ethical issues and ensure that the findings' validity will be respected. Blowing off any one of these steps can cause opt-in rates to plummet and undermine a program for years.

Here's your playbook for the ethical, smart use of employee data:

Opt In

It starts with one of the simplest and oldest privacy guidelines: If you launch a program collecting new kinds of data, requiring employees to opt in to it (and leaving out all who don't) is essential. Forcing people to give up data about themselves at work may be strictly legal in the United States and several other countries, but that is not the case globally. Regulations such as GDPR, while not explicitly focused on the workplace, do spell out restrictions that would make data collection difficult for a multinational organization.

But even in jurisdictions that permit it, coerced monitoring or requiring employees to opt out (especially if the choice is obscured by, say, being buried in the fine print during onboarding) opens many ethical and business concerns. First and foremost, it may backfire from a purely economic perspective. Groundbreaking research by Harvard Business School's Ethan Bernstein has shown that when employees feel that everything they do is completely transparent, the result is often reduced performance. And when competition for talent is intense, workers may leave companies that compel them to give up their data. Beyond that, firms face reputational risk. For example, Amazon, Tesco, and the *Daily Telegraph* all experienced weeks of negative media coverage for their proposed or poorly executed monitoring efforts. Some of those programs were very well intended: The *Telegraph*'s was aimed at improving energy efficiency—something few employees would probably object to—through the use of desk sensors. But the media company rushed the rollout and provided little information to its employees before foisting the sensors on them. It was forced to quickly withdraw them after hard internal pushback and skewering in the media.

Setting up an opt-in program is challenging and time-intensive in the short term. The program must include strong protections for employees who choose not to participate so that they don't feel coerced or penalized. Chief among those protections is data aggregation to prevent individuals' behavior from being identified. But I also advise further precautions, such as consent forms and data anonymization at the source of collection (so overeager, curious-to-a-fault managers can't snoop on the minute-by-minute activities of employees).

To design opt-in consent forms that are clear, concise, and easy to understand, companies should take their cue from internal review boards (IRBs) at universities, which have stringent procedures for how researchers interact with human subjects. On IRB forms, researchers must clearly specify what data is collected and how it will be used. Employees should be provided with appendices that spell out the specific database tables that will be populated, so they can see exactly what kind of information will be stored. Finally, companies also need to sign the forms, creating legally binding contracts with employees.

Communication and Transparency

Blindly sending out consent forms to all employees and hoping for high opt-in rates isn't a winning strategy. The rollout of ethical people analytics involves lots of communication and constant transparency. I approach it like this:

- *Week one:* An introductory email lays out the promise of the proposed analytics program, providing a summary of the company's approach and goals and links to news articles about similar programs.

- *Week two:* Managers attend an informational session about the technology and are given time to ask questions and raise concerns. They then meet with their own teams to describe the program and field any questions from their reports.

- *Week three:* The CEO holds a town hall in which the company shares the materials given to managers with the entire staff, encouraging everyone to speak freely about concerns and to ask any questions.

In some cases companies have opted to compensate workers for participating in analytics programs, either with small amounts of money or rewards such as Amazon gift cards or company T-shirts. However, in my experience this is problematic and ineffective. For one, it gives the employer specific information about who's participating. But these incentives also typically yield no measurable increase in participation. Employees seem to feel that payment for their data means they're signing away their right to privacy, which produces a more negative reaction. *If they have to pay me to participate, they must be taking a lot, and who knows what they're doing with it?* seems to be the thinking.

With all programs, managers should prepare for a backlash. Emotional reactions, tough questions, and accusations are common even with well-intentioned monitoring. Expecting reasonably universal buy-in is a mistake, because employees not only need to understand exactly what's being done but must trust managers' assurances that the company is being honest and open. In cultures where trust or morale is low, this is a massive hurdle. Simply telling employees you will behave responsibly isn't good enough; you have to show them with completely transparent program operations.

Often as I learn about people analytics initiatives in other organizations, I discover that companies intentionally withhold information from workers about what data's being collected and why. Companies naively assume that these practices won't be discovered by employees, but they often are. Doing something legal but unethical tends to incur a severe backlash. There are many examples of this in the marketplace, and typically companies that engage in unethical monitoring behaviors suffer both internal and external consequences.

Aggregation

Companies often assume that data becomes anonymous when you detach a name from it. It doesn't. Because human behavior is unique, it's possible to identify people in data without their names, particularly with communication network data.

Imagine Anna has a private office and a Bluetooth beacon on her ID tag that detects her precise location in the office at all times. Anna is a workaholic. If we showed data on how each worker spent time in the office without revealing anyone's name, we would likely see that one person spent much more time there than anyone else did. That would be Anna, and she and everyone who works with her would know that beyond any doubt. That's just a simplified example involving a single type of data. In fact, data analysis and machine learning allow us to identify individuals with less obvious data. For instance, it's extremely easy to identify individual people through their location patterns, and semantic analysis can determine with high probability who the author of a text is, just by recognizing the author's language habits.

Company-issued cell phones are often used for location tracking, but they can be problematic. If only data associated with the office is collected, the phone effectively is just like an ID tag. In practice, however, information on employees' whereabouts when outside the office may be logged and collected. That data, besides having quite limited business applications, is extremely sensitive and should be avoided.

Steering clear of these pitfalls isn't difficult, and it's actually beneficial. For, beyond creating privacy risks, analyzing the behavior of individuals or singling out one person for tracking is a methodologically inferior approach to data analysis. Why?

- *Contextual differences.* Someone may behave in a certain way because of his or her distinctive situation. When searching for the traits of high performers, for example, a company may look at a single star employee and notice the data shows that he works over lunch. Does that mean high performers are more likely to be lunchtime workers? It's impossible to tell from one person! Maybe this employee has to meet with a large group over lunch because he needs 10 people to approve decisions and that's the only time everyone can meet to review them. If no other decision tasks have that structure, it's unlikely that working lunches alone are the cause of high performance.

- *Privacy violations.* There is an undeniable Big Brother aspect to microanalyzing the behavior of individuals. Even if such an analysis produced a benefit, it would be dwarfed by the negative reaction employees would inevitably, legitimately display: The probable increase in turnover, decrease in performance, and bad publicity a company would experience would not be worth it.

Instead of individual data, companies should ask their analytics teams to report aggregate data: group averages or correlations. Given that companies should care about distributions of behavior and not individuals' patterns, this practice also fits nicely with organizational needs.

Look Beyond the Numbers

No matter how sophisticated a company's data gathering is, it will be useless if the firm doesn't measure the right things.

For example, while it's natural to think that the content of communication is more important to examine than communication patterns, that's not true. At a company we advised, my team and I found that top management communicated with one division fewer than five hours a month. That division had more than 10,000 employees and was responsible for over 10% of the company's revenue. Not surprisingly, it was consistently underperforming and not strategically aligned with the organization. The exact substance of the small number of conversations that did occur was immaterial. The bigger issue was that management rarely talked with people in the division. We could confidently predict that if management simply had *more* communication with them, it would boost the division's performance.

It's also important to keep in mind that no algorithm or data set, no matter how complete or advanced, will be able to capture the entire complexity of work. And you shouldn't try to build such an algorithm or, worse, buy into a consultant who promises one. People within the organization already have an understanding of the work's complete scope. Casting that aside in favor of blindly following an algorithm will lead to many stupid decisions. Contextual, qualitative information helps organizations understand how to weight quantitative metrics.

I remember one case in which an engineering organization wanted to use behavioral data to improve team performance. In such situations, a metric like *cohesion* (group strength, gathered from chat and sensor data) is often correlated with higher performance. A pilot showed that increasing cohesion helped teams hit their key performance indicator, on-time delivery. Looking at those results alone, management thought it would roll out policies to increase cohesion across all teams. That would have been an error. After all, some teams were trying to invent radically new products. Management should expect them to miss their milestones more frequently than other teams, because their timelines are harder to estimate. Applying the cohesion algorithm there wouldn't have been optimal. Other behaviors, like exploration (interacting more with other teams), predicted their success better. So if the company had blindly set up programs to increase cohesion across all teams, it would have reduced the performance of the ones focused on innovation.

My colleagues and I encounter this problem all the time, and because of it we make sure to work with internal stakeholders to understand why one group's data analysis won't always apply to another's. Their deep contextual knowledge points us to what data collection and analysis matter for each part of the organization.

The potential of people analytics to improve decision-making is astounding. It can help workers like their jobs better, make more money, and spend more time with their families. In Japan, for example, monitoring technology is starting to be used to reduce the tremendous human cost of overwork. While in the past companies there would implement a workload reduction program and consider it a success if after a year no one had committed suicide, today they're able to see immediately whether workloads are actually reduced. Rather than continuing to do something ineffective, they can quickly figure out what will improve their work environments and adjust. This literally saves lives.

However, companies have a responsibility to avoid succumbing to using analytics for outcomes workers may blanch at. Firms need to start putting protections in place today. If they don't, a wave of overreactive legislation will hit them; you can even see the glimmerings of one in GDPR. That may wipe out people analytics' enormous potential for good. So it's incumbent upon the analytics industry and companies to advocate for strong protections too. The stakes are too high not to.

Originally published in September 2018. Reprint H04J6Z

Don't Let Metrics Undermine Your Business

by Michael Harris and Bill Tayler

TYING PERFORMANCE METRICS TO STRATEGY has become an accepted best practice over the past few decades. Strategy is abstract by definition, but metrics give strategy form, allowing our minds to grasp it more readily. With metrics, Ford Motor Company's onetime strategy "Quality is job one" could be translated into Six Sigma performance standards. Apple's "Think different" and Samsung's "Create the future" could be linked to the amount of sales from new products. If strategy is the blueprint for building an organization, metrics are the concrete, wood, drywall, and bricks.

But there's a hidden trap in this organizational architecture: A company can easily lose sight of its strategy and instead focus strictly on the metrics that are meant to *represent* it. For an extreme example of this problem, look to Wells Fargo, where employees opened 3.5 million deposit and credit card accounts without customers' consent in an effort to implement its now-infamous "cross-selling" strategy.

The costs from that debacle were enormous, and the bank has yet to see the end of the financial carnage. In addition to paying initial fines ($185 million), reimbursing customers for fees ($6.1 million), and eventually settling a class-action lawsuit to cover damages as far back as 2002 ($142 million), Wells Fargo has faced strong headwinds in attracting new retail customers. In April 2017, it reported that first-quarter credit card applications were down 42% year over year, with new checking-account openings down 35%. Meanwhile, more revelations about unauthorized mortgage modifications and fees, improper auto loan practices, and other missteps surfaced throughout 2017. In the fourth quarter the bank had to set aside a $3.25 billion accrual for future litigation expenses. In February 2018 the Federal Reserve prohibited Wells Fargo from growing its assets any further until it strengthened its governance and risk management. This was followed in April by a joint $1 billion fine from the Consumer Financial Protection Bureau (CFPB) and the Office of the Comptroller of the Currency (OCC), which led Wells Fargo to increase its litigation accrual by $800 million. While press releases from the CFPB and the OCC tie the agencies' action only to mortgage fees and auto loan problems, the political context suggests that the penalty's severity stems in part from public outrage over the original fake-accounts scandal. In the face of the bank's prolonged difficulties, the CEO who'd taken the helm after the scandal, Timothy Sloan, resigned in March 2019.

Were these devastating outcomes simply the natural consequences of having a bad strategy? Closer examination suggests that Wells Fargo never actually had a cross-selling *strategy*. It had a cross-selling *metric*. In its third quarter 2016 earnings report, the bank mentions an effort to "best align our cross-sell *metric* with our *strategic focus* of long-term retail banking relationships" [emphasis added]. In other words, Wells Fargo had—and still has—a strategy of building long-term customer relationships, and management intended to track the degree to which it was accomplishing that goal by measuring cross-selling. With brutal irony, a focus on the metric unraveled many of the bank's valuable long-term relationships.

Every day, across almost every organization, strategy is being hijacked by numbers, just as it was at Wells Fargo. It turns out that the tendency to mentally replace strategy with metrics—called *surrogation*—is quite pervasive. And it can destroy company value.

Idea in Brief

The Problem

Companies that work hard on their strategies and carefully monitor their progress often run into spectacular trouble.

Why It Happens

People have a behavioral tendency—known as surrogation—to confuse what's being measured with the metric being used.

How to Fix It

To reduce the risk of surrogation, make sure that the people executing your strategy had a role in formulating it, don't link incentives too tightly to strategy metrics, and use multiple metrics to assess performance.

The Surrogation Snare

Of course, we all know that metrics are inherently imperfect at some level. In business the intent behind metrics is usually to capture some underlying intangible goal—and they almost always fail to do this as well as we would like. Your performance management system is full of metrics that are flawed proxies for what you care about.

Here's a common scenario: A company selects "delighting the customer" as a strategic objective and decides to track progress on it using customer survey scores. The surveys do tell managers something about how well the firm is pleasing customers, but somehow employees start thinking the strategy is to maximize survey scores, rather than to deliver a great customer experience.

It's easy to see how this could quickly become a problem, because there are plenty of ways to boost scores while actually displeasing customers. For example, what happened the last time you were urged to rate your experience a 10 on a satisfaction survey "because anything but a 10 is considered a failure"? That request may have turned negative feedback into a nonresponse or an artificially high score, and the pressure was probably off-putting. And think about all the pop-up windows, follow-up emails, and robocalls that pester you with surveys you would rather ignore. Such tactics tend to lower a customer's satisfaction with a company, but surrogation can lead those charged with delighting the customer to use them *despite* the strategy.

Surrogation is especially harmful when the metric and the strategy are poorly aligned. The greater the mismatch, the larger the potential damage. When a production manager's success at achieving the strategic objective "make high-quality products" is measured by using very precise quality standards (such as "ball bearings must be 10 millimeters in diameter, plus or minus 0.0001 millimeters"), surrogation might not be a problem. However, if success at the objective is measured by the number of customer returns, the production manager might find creative ways to avoid returns. For example, he or she might connect directly with the purchasing departments of clientele, offering to personally handle any product concerns so that returns are registered as rework rather than returns. Or the manager might be willing to gamble a bit, pushing beyond acceptable (or even safe) quality standards, knowing that while the lower quality will increase the likelihood of a return, it may not actually trigger one. Furthermore, when a single metric is used more widely—for example, to gauge the performance of multiple managers overseeing various components of a complex product—surrogation can have a far bigger impact and do much greater harm.

What Happened at Wells Fargo

Several explanations have been provided for how things went awry at Wells Fargo. The most widely accepted theory lays the blame on the company's incentive system. In the words of Richard Cordray, the former CFPB director involved in imposing an early fine on the bank: "What happened here . . . is that Wells Fargo built an incentive-compensation program that made it possible for its employees to pursue underhanded sales practices."

But was the compensation approach actually the root of Wells Fargo's problems—or was it simply a symptom of a more insidious ailment? Another culprit might have been the combination of challenging sales quotas and relentless pressure to meet them.

Indeed, employees under investigation cited pressure more often than incentives as a cause for misconduct. Another possible cause was a permissive sales culture. A key finding of an internal investigation was that management espoused the philosophy that "it was acceptable to sell 10 low-quality accounts to realize one good one." The investigation found that managers referred to products that the customer did not need (or want) as "slippage" and that a certain amount of slippage was deemed "the cost of doing business in any retail environment." But again, sales pressure and questionable culture could merely have been symptoms of a more pervasive and pernicious problem.

Incentives, pressure to meet quotas, and sales culture were all tied to a system employed throughout Wells Fargo at the time. In fact, it's one found at almost every company. It's the performance measurement system, used to monitor everyday business activities, from the organizational level on down to the individual-employee level. There could be no sales incentives at Wells Fargo without rigorous *tracking* of sales numbers. There would have been no accounts-per-household goals, pressure to meet them, or culture surrounding them if customers' accounts were never *counted*. Ex-CEO John Stumpf's now-infamous mantra, "Eight is great" (the goal was to have eight Wells Fargo products per customer), was based on this common denominator.

The real source of Wells Fargo's problems was measurement. When the bank decided to actively track daily cross-sales numbers, employees rationally responded by working to maximize them. Throw in financial incentives, a permissive culture, and intense demands for performance, and they might even illegally open some unauthorized accounts, all in the name of advancing the "strategy" of cross-selling.

Don't get us wrong. We're not suggesting that measurement is a bad thing. It's not, and there's a reason it's ubiquitous in business: It's the only way we can make sense of our environment, our results, and our strategic objectives, which we must do if we are to succeed. Metrics provide clearly defined direction where strategy

The Biggest Surrogation of All?

IF YOU STOP TO THINK ABOUT IT, the surrogation trap is everywhere. Even the most common performance metric—earnings—was conceived as a proxy for something bigger and more abstract: Hicksian income.

Don't remember learning about Hicksian income in your accounting class? That's probably because you didn't take accounting in the mid-1900s, when our ideas about measuring value began to congeal. John Hicks described this fairly abstract metric as the amount of money that can be distributed to shareholders while still leaving the company's value unchanged. In contemporary terms, it's the value added by a company's operations. Earnings were a clearly defined proxy for that value and were intended to make an abstract concept more concrete. But generating accounting earnings isn't necessarily the same thing as creating value. After all, financial statements don't present a complete picture of what's happening in companies, especially if the numbers in them are manipulated. And investors who surrogate may support financial decisions that do not create value, such as cost cuts that undermine customer service and long-term financial performance.

While there is no formal evidence that investors surrogate, the outsize market reactions we see when a company misses an earnings target by a penny suggest that many are falling into the trap.

---

may otherwise seem too amorphous to have an impact. Because they can coordinate behaviors and actions, metrics are crucial. But as the Wells Fargo case shows, unless the inherent distortions of metrics are understood, they can be dangerous—and the distortions can be amplified precisely because the flawed metrics coordinate behaviors.

Guarding Against Surrogation

To prevent surrogation, we must first understand how it happens. Two recent studies on surrogation—one using fMRI machines to measure blood flow in the brain to better understand how people make decisions, and the other using video games to examine surrogation in a nonbusiness setting—suggest that surrogation is a common subconscious bias: Whenever metrics are present, people tend to surrogate. Nobel prize winner Daniel Kahneman and Yale professor Shane Frederick postulate that three conditions are necessary to produce the type of substitution we see with surrogation:

1. The objective or strategy is fairly abstract.

2. The metric of the strategy is concrete and conspicuous.

3. The employee accepts, at least subconsciously, the substitution of the metric for the strategy.

Multiple research studies have helped demonstrate how these conditions combine to produce surrogation. Knowledge of them supplies us with the means to combat the problem. Just as fire is stifled when the heat, fuel, or oxygen necessary for combustion is removed, surrogation can be suppressed by cutting off one or more of its key ingredients. Here's how to do that:

Get the people responsible for implementing strategy to help formulate it

This helps reduce surrogation because those involved in executing the strategy will then be better able to grasp it, despite its abstract nature—and to avoid replacing it with metrics. It's particularly crucial to bring the executives and senior managers who are charged with communicating strategy into this process. Research that one of us, Bill, did with Willie Choi of the University of Wisconsin and Gary Hecht of the University of Illinois, Urbana-Champaign, suggests that simply *talking* about strategy with people is not sufficient. In other words you can't just invite them to boardroom briefings and hang signs around the building promoting the strategy—you need to involve people in its development.

Consider the experiences of one organization Bill advised, Intermountain Healthcare. Its goal is to provide high-quality, low-cost care. One of the battlegrounds for this type of "value-based care" is the treatment of lower back pain. It turns out that most lower back pain goes away on its own in a few weeks. Medication and surgery can help, but they can also hurt—and they can be very costly. The data suggests that once a patient presents with lower back pain, the ideal response is to wait. So, with the involvement and advice of practicing physicians, Intermountain recently formulated a strategy aimed at reducing unnecessary interventions. To measure performance on the strategy, Intermountain began tracking whether doctors waited at least four weeks after meeting with a patient with lower back pain to recommend an X-ray, MRI, or another, more invasive diagnosis or treatment method.

The danger with this metric, of course, is that doctors could begin to see "make patients wait" as the objective rather than providing high-quality care at low cost. But because Intermountain doctors helped develop the strategy, this type of surrogation was far less likely to happen. And because the physicians were also heavily involved in the rollout and training for the strategy and its metrics, they could help others avoid surrogation as well. Indeed, Nick Bassett, executive director of population health at Intermountain, says that "without question, when physicians are involved in designing objectives, they better understand those objectives, and when they understand the objectives, they have proven time and time again their ability to determine the right course of action, often in spite of a particular metric."

Brett Muse, a doctor at Intermountain who played a large part in the strategy's development and rollout, agrees. "When I get in front of physicians and throw data at them, they get glassy-eyed," he says. Instead, he gets in front of the group and says, "Here's a problem involving quality of care. Let's try to solve this problem—and by the way, here's some data we can look at to see how we're doing."

Loosen the link between metrics and incentives

Tying compensation to a metric-based target tends to increase surrogation—an unfortunate side effect of pay for performance. Besides tapping into any monetary motivations people might have, this approach makes the metric much more visible, which means employees are more likely to focus on it at the expense of the strategy.

To think about how to get around this problem, let's look again at Intermountain's lower-back-pain metric. If management had done the obvious and just informed physicians that they would be paid a small bonus each time they required a patient to wait four weeks before receiving any costly tests or treatments, it probably would have driven even the most well-meaning doctors away from the true strategy of reducing unnecessary interventions and toward maximization of the metric. But the people overseeing the program didn't tie compensation to the metric, because they recognized that most doctors are already intrinsically motivated to provide high-value care. In addition, they set the target for the percentage of patients who waited four weeks before medical intervention at 80%. This served as a reminder to doctors that high-quality, low-cost care for *most* patients meant waiting for lower back pain to resolve itself, but for some patients—for example, those who waited a month before seeing the doctor in the first place—immediate treatment was warranted. The target reflected the imperfect nature of the metric and drew physicians' attention back to the underlying strategy.

Use multiple metrics

Another study Bill did with Choi and Hecht shows that people surrogate less when they're compensated for meeting targets on multiple metrics of a strategy rather than just one. This approach highlights the fact that no single metric completely captures the strategy, which makes people more likely to consciously reject substituting it for the strategy. At Intermountain overall physician performance is assessed with a myriad of metrics, including patient satisfaction, condition-specific quality metrics (such as average A1C levels of diabetes patients), health outcomes (such as hospital readmittance), preventive efforts (such as appropriately timed mammograms), and total cost of care. No lone metric is used to quantify the competence or contribution of the medical staff. Multiple yardsticks do add complexity to the task of performance evaluation, but they're essential to keeping people focused on the true strategy and avoiding surrogation.

Wells Fargo Revisited

To see if Wells Fargo remains vulnerable to surrogation, let's look at the actions it has taken in the wake of its crisis. As far as we can tell, the bank is heading in the right direction with its damage-control efforts.

First, the new management's emphasis on rebuilding trust with customers after the scandal has made the long-term relationship strategy much more clear and prominent. Second, the bank has stopped paying employees to cross-sell and has eliminated all sales goals. That may sound extreme, but it was appropriate for Wells Fargo because an obsession with sales quotas had become so entrenched at the bank. To address that issue, the cross-selling metric and everything related to it needed to go. Finally, Wells Fargo now gauges strategic success using at least a dozen metrics related to its customer focus, emphasizing that no single number tells the whole story and encouraging employees to consciously reject surrogation.

That progress notwithstanding, this episode in Wells Fargo's history was devastating in terms of both quantifiable out-of-pocket costs and less measurable (but truly colossal) reputational costs, and there's no indication yet that the bank is close to full recovery. However, at the very least, the new steps Wells Fargo has taken seem likely to remind tomorrow's managers and employees that performance metrics are mere representations of strategy, not the strategy itself.

———————

Many managers learn the hard way that surrogation can spoil strategy, and if you don't take action to protect against it, it's very likely that sooner or later personal experience will lead you to the same realization. If you're using performance metrics, surrogation is probably already happening—the mere presence of a metric, even absent any compensation, is enough to induce some level of the behavior. So it's time to take a hard look internally to see which metrics might be most prone to surrogation and consider where it might cause the most damage. As the Wells Fargo case illustrates, preventing the disease is far preferable to treating its symptoms.

Originally published in September–October 2019. Reprint R1905C

"Numbers Take Us Only So Far"

by Maxine Williams

I WAS ONCE EVICTED FROM AN APARTMENT because I was Black. I had secured a lovely place on the banks of Lake Geneva through an agent and therefore hadn't met the owner in person before signing the lease. Once my family and I moved in and the color of my skin was clear to see, the landlady asked us to leave. If she had known that I was Black, I was told, she would never have rented to me.

Terrible as it felt at the time, her directness was useful to me. It meant I didn't have to scour the facts looking for some other, non-racist rationale for her sudden rejection.

Many people have been denied housing, bank loans, jobs, promotions, and more because of their race. But they're rarely told that's the reason, as I was—particularly in the workplace. For one thing, such discrimination is illegal. For another, executives tend to think—and have a strong desire to believe—that they're hiring and promoting people fairly when they aren't. (Research shows that individuals who view themselves as objective are often the ones who apply the most unconscious bias.) Though managers don't cite or (usually) even perceive race as a factor in their decisions, they use ambiguous assessment criteria to filter out people who aren't like them, research by Kellogg professor Lauren Rivera shows. People in marginalized racial and ethnic groups are deemed more often than whites to be "not the right cultural fit" or "not ready" for high-level roles; they're taken out of the running because their "communication style" is somehow off the mark. They're left only with lingering suspicions that their identity is the real issue, especially when decision-makers' bias is masked by good intentions.

I work in the field of diversity. I've also been Black my whole life. So I know that underrepresented people in the workplace yearn for two things: The first is to hear that they're not crazy to suspect, at times, that there's a connection between negative treatment and bias. The second is to be offered institutional support.

The first need has a clear path to fulfillment. When we encounter colleagues or friends who have been mistreated and who believe that their identity may be the reason, we should acknowledge that it's fair to be suspicious. There's no leap of faith here—numerous studies show how pervasive such bias still is.

But how can we address the second need? In an effort to find valid, scalable ways to counteract or reverse bias and promote diversity, organizations are turning to people analytics—a relatively new field in business operations and talent management that replaces gut decisions with data-driven practices. People analytics aspires to be evidence-based. And for some HR issues—such as figuring out how many job interviews are needed to assess a candidate, or determining how employees' work commutes affect their job satisfaction—it is. Statistically significant findings have led to some big changes in organizations. Unfortunately, companies that try to apply analytics to the challenges of underrepresented groups at work often complain that the relevant data sets don't include enough people to produce reliable insights—the sample size, the n, is too small. Basically they're saying, "If only there were more of you, we could tell you why there are so few of you."

Companies have access to more data than they realize, however. To supplement a small n, they can venture out and look at the larger context in which they operate. But data volume alone won't give leaders the insight they need to increase diversity in their organizations. They must also take a closer look at the individuals from underrepresented groups who work for them—those who barely register on the analytics radar.

Idea in Brief

Though executives tend to think they're hiring and promoting fairly, bias still creeps into their decisions. They often use ambiguous criteria to filter out people who aren't like them or deem people from underrepresented groups to be "not the right cultural fit," leaving those employees with the uneasy feeling that their identity might be the real issue.

Companies need to acknowledge that it's fair for employees from underrepresented groups to be suspicious about bias, says Maxine Williams. They also must find ways to give those workers more support. Many organizations are turning to people analytics, which aspires to replace gut decisions with data-driven ones. Unfortunately, firms often say that they don't have enough people from marginalized groups in their data sets to produce reliable insights.

Employers must supplement small n's: draw on industry or sector data; learn from what's happening in other companies; and deeply examine the experiences of individuals who work for them by talking with them to gather critical qualitative information. If firms are systematic and comprehensive in these efforts, they'll have a better chance of improving diversity and inclusion.

Supplementing the N

Nonprofit research organizations are doing important work that sheds light on how bias shapes hiring and advancement in various industries and sectors. For example, a study by the Ascend Foundation showed that in 2013 white men and white women in five major Silicon Valley firms were 154% more likely to become executives than their Asian counterparts were. And though both race and gender were factors in the glass ceiling for Asians, race had 3.7 times the impact that gender did.

It took two more years of research and analysis—using data on several hundred thousand employees, drawn from the EEOC's aggregation of all Bay Area technology firms and from the individual reports of 13 U.S. tech companies—before Ascend determined how bias affected the prospects of Blacks and Hispanics. Among those groups it again found that, overall, race had a greater negative impact than gender on advancement from the professional to the executive level. In the Bay Area white women fared worse than white men but much better than all Asians, Hispanics, and Blacks. Minority women faced the biggest obstacle to entering the executive ranks. Black and Hispanic women were severely challenged by both their low numbers at the professional level and their lower chances of rising from professional to executive. Asian women, who had more representation at the professional level than other minorities, had the lowest chances of moving up from professional to executive. An analysis of national data found similar results.

By analyzing industry or sector data on underrepresented groups—and examining patterns in hiring, promotions, and other decisions about talent—we can better manage the problems and risks in our own organizations. Tech companies may look at the Ascend reports and say, "Hey, let's think about what's happening with our competitors' talent. There's a good chance it's happening here, too." Their HR teams might then add a layer of career tracking for women of color, for example, or create training programs for managing diverse teams.

Another approach is to extrapolate lessons from other companies' analyses. We might look, for instance, at Red Ventures, a Charlotte-based digital media company. Red Ventures is diverse by several measures. (It has a Latino CEO, and about 40% of its employees are people of color.) But that doesn't mean there aren't problems to solve. When I met with its top executives, they told me they had recently done an analysis of performance reviews at the firm and found that internalized stereotypes were having a negative effect on Black and Latino employees' self-assessments. On average, members of those two groups rated their performance 30% lower than their managers did (whereas white male employees scored their performance 10% higher than their managers did). The study also uncovered a correlation between racial isolation and negative self-perception. For example, people of color who worked in engineering generally rated themselves lower than those who worked in sales, where there were more Blacks and Latinos. These patterns were consistent at all levels, from junior to senior staff.

In response, the HR team at Red Ventures trained employees in how to do self-assessments, and that has started to close the gap for Blacks and Latinos (who more recently rated themselves 22% lower than their managers did). Hallie Cornetta, the company's VP of human capital, explained that the training "focused on the importance of completing quantitative and qualitative self-assessments honestly, in a way that shows how employees personally view their performance across our five key dimensions, rather than how they assume their manager or peers view their performance." She added: "We then shared tangible examples of what 'exceptional' versus 'solid' versus 'needs improvement' looks like in these dimensions to remove some of the subjectivity and help minority—and all—employees assess with greater direction and confidence."

Getting Personal

Once we've gone broader by supplementing the n, we can go deeper by examining individual cases. This is critical. Algorithms and statistics do not capture what it feels like to be the only Black or Hispanic team member or the effect that marginalization has on individual employees and the group as a whole. We must talk openly with people, one-on-one, to learn about their experiences with bias, and share our own stories to build trust and make the topic safe for discussion. What we discover through those conversations is every bit as important as what shows up in the aggregated data.

An industry colleague, who served as a lead on diversity at a tech company, broke it down for me like this: "When we do our employee surveys, the Latinos always say they are happy. But I'm Latino, and I know that we are often hesitant to rock the boat. Saying the truth is too risky, so we'll say what you want to hear—even if you sit us down in a focus group. I also know that those aggregated numbers where there are enough of us for the n to be significant don't reflect the heterogeneity in our community. Someone who is light-skinned and grew up in Latin America in an upper-middle-class family probably is very happy and comfortable indeed. Someone who is darker-skinned and grew up working-class in America is probably not feeling that same sense of belonging. I'm going to spend time and effort trying to build solutions for the ones I know are at a disadvantage, whether the data tells me that there's a problem with all Latinos or not."

This is a recurring theme. I spoke with 10 diversity and HR professionals at companies with head counts ranging from 60 to 300,000, all of whom are working on programs or interventions for the people who don't register as "big" in big data. They rely at least somewhat on their own intuition when exploring the impact of marginalization. This may seem counter to the mission of people analytics, which is to remove personal perspective and gut feelings from the talent equation entirely. But to discover the effects of bias in our organizations—and to identify complicating factors within groups, such as class and colorism among Latinos and others—we need to collect and analyze qualitative data, too. Intuition can help us find it. The diversity and HR folks described using their "spidey sense" or knowing there is "something in the water"—essentially, understanding that bias is probably a factor, even though people analytics doesn't always prove causes and predict outcomes. Through conversations with employees—and sometimes through focus groups, if the resources are there and participants feel it's safe to be honest—they reality-check what their instincts tell them, often drawing on their own experiences with bias. One colleague said, "The combination of qualitative and quantitative data is ideal, but at the end of the day there is nothing that data will tell us that we don't already know as Black people. I know what my experience was as an African American man who worked for 16 years in roles that weren't related to improving diversity. It's as much heart as head in this work."

A Call to Action

The proposition at the heart of people analytics is sound—if you want to hire and manage fairly, gut-based decisions are not enough. However, we have to create a new approach, one that also works for small data sets—for the marginalized and the underrepresented.

Here are my recommendations:

First, analysts must challenge the traditional minimum confident n, pushing themselves to look beyond the limited hard data. They don't have to prove that the difference in performance ratings between Blacks and whites is "statistically significant" to help managers understand the impact of bias in performance reviews. We already know from the breadth and depth of social science research about bias that it is pervasive in the workplace and influences ratings, so we can combine those insights with what we hear and see on the ground and simply start operating as if bias exists in our companies. We may have to place a higher value on the experiences shared by five or 10 employees—or look more carefully at the descriptive data, such as head counts for underrepresented groups and average job satisfaction scores cut by race and gender—to examine the impact of bias at a more granular level.

In addition, analysts should frequently provide confidence intervals—that is, guidance on how much managers can trust the data if the n's are too small to prove statistical significance. When managers get that information, they're more likely to make changes in their hiring and management practices, even if they believe—as most do—that they are already treating people fairly. Suppose, for example, that as Red Ventures began collecting data on self-assessments, analysts had a 75% confidence level that Blacks and Latinos were underrating themselves. The analysts could then have advised managers to go to their minority direct reports, examine the results from that performance period, and determine together whether the self-reviews truly reflected their contributions. It's a simple but collaborative way to address implicit bias or stereotyping that you're reasonably sure is there while giving agency to each employee.

Second, companies also need to be more consistent and comprehensive in their qualitative analysis. Many already conduct interviews and focus groups to gain insights on the challenges of the underrepresented; some even do textual analysis of written performance reviews, exit interview notes, and hiring memos, looking for language that signals bias or negative stereotyping. But we have to go further. We need to find a viable way to create and process more-objective performance evaluations, given the internalized biases of both employees and managers, and to determine how those biases affect ratings.

This journey begins with educating all employees on the real-life impact of bias and negative stereotypes. At Facebook we offer a variety of training programs with an emphasis on spotting and counteracting bias, and we keep reinforcing key messages post-training, since we know these muscles take time to build. We issue reminders at critical points to shape decision-making and behavior. For example, in our performance evaluation tool, we incorporate prompts for people to check word choice when writing reviews and self-assessments. We remind them, for instance, that terms like "cultural fit" can allow bias to creep in and that they should avoid describing women as "bossy" if they wouldn't describe men who demonstrated the same behaviors that way. We don't yet have data on how this is influencing the language used—it's a new intervention—but we will be examining patterns over time.

Perhaps above all, HR and analytics departments must value both qualitative and quantitative expertise and apply mixed-method approaches everywhere possible. At Facebook we're building cross-functional teams with both types of specialists, because no single research method can fully capture the complex layers of bias that everyone brings to the workplace. We view all research methods as trying to solve the same problem from different angles. Sometimes we approach challenges from a quantitative perspective first, to uncover the "what" before looking to the qualitative experts to dive into the "why" and "how." For instance, if the numbers showed that certain teams were losing or attracting minority employees at higher rates than others (the "what"), we might conduct interviews, run focus groups, or analyze text from company surveys to understand the "why," and pull out themes or lessons for other parts of the company. In other scenarios we might reverse the order of those steps. For example, if we repeatedly heard from members of one social group that they weren't seeing their peers getting recognized at the same rate as people in other groups, we could then investigate whether numerical trends confirmed those observations, or conduct statistical analyses to figure out which organizational circumstances were associated with employees' being more or less likely to get recognized.

Cross-functional teams also help us reap the benefits of cognitive diversity. Working together stretches everyone, challenging team members' own assumptions and biases. Getting to absolute "whys" and "hows" on any issue, from recruitment to engagement to performance, is always going to be tough. But we believe that with this approach, we stand the best chance of making improvements across the company. As we analyze the results of Facebook's Pulse survey, given twice a year to employees, and review Performance Summary Cycle inputs, we'll continue to look for signs of problems as well as progress.

Evidence of discrimination or unfair outcomes may not be as certain or obvious in the workplace as it was for me the time I was evicted from my apartment. But we can increase our certainty, and it's essential that we do so. The underrepresented people at our companies are not crazy to perceive biases working against them, and they can get institutional support.

Originally published in November–December 2017. **Reprint** R1706L

Managers Can't Do It All

by Diane Gherson and Lynda Gratton

JENNIFER STARES AT HER UPWARD-FEEDBACK REPORT and wonders how she got to this point. How could a veteran like her, someone who was once celebrated as manager of the year, receive such negative ratings? She used to enjoy her role, but now everything feels out of control. Her job has been reshaped so constantly—by sweeping process reengineering, digitization, and agile initiatives, and most recently by remote work—that she always feels at least one step behind.

The amount of change that has taken place in just the past few years is overwhelming. The management layer above her was eliminated, which doubled the size of her team, and almost half the people on it are now working on cross-division projects led by *other* managers. She and her team used to meet in her office for progress reviews, but now she has no office, and if she wants to know how her people are doing, she has to join their stand-ups, which makes her feel like an onlooker rather than their boss. She no longer feels in touch with how everybody is doing, and yet she has the same set of personnel responsibilities as before: providing performance feedback, making salary adjustments, hiring and firing, engaging in career discussions.

Not only that, but she's being asked to take on even more. Because her company is rapidly digitizing, for example, she's responsible for upgrading her staff's technical skills. This makes her uncomfortable because it feels threatening to many of her team members. When she talks with them about it, she's expected to demonstrate endless amounts of empathy—something that has never been her strong suit. She's supposed to seek out diverse talent and create a climate of psychological safety while simultaneously downsizing the unit. She understands why all these things are important, but they're not what she signed up for when she became a manager, and she's just not sure that she has the emotional energy to handle them.

What happened to the stable, well-defined job that she was so good at for so long? What happened to the power and status that used to come with that job? Is *she* the problem? Is she simply no longer able to keep up with the demands of the evolving workplace? Is she now part of the "frozen middle"—the much-maligned layer of management that obstructs change rather than enables it?

Jennifer—a composite of several real people we have met in our work—has no answers to these questions. All she knows is that she's frustrated, unhappy, and overwhelmed.

As are managers everywhere.

One of us, Lynda, is an academic researcher and consultant to corporations, and the other, Diane, was until her recent retirement the chief human resources officer at IBM (in which she still owns stock). In those roles we have closely observed the changing job of the manager, and we can report that a crisis is looming.

The signs are everywhere. In 2021, when we asked executives from 60 companies around the world how their managers were doing, we got unanimous reports of frustration and exhaustion. Similarly, when the research firm Gartner asked 75 HR leaders from companies worldwide how their managers were faring, 68% reported that they were overwhelmed. Nonetheless, according to Gartner, only 14% of those companies had taken steps to help alleviate their managers' burdens.

The problem isn't hard to diagnose. The traditional role of the manager evolved in the hierarchical workplaces of the industrial age, but in our fluid, flatter, postindustrial age that role is beginning to look archaic.

The irony is that we actually need great people leaders more than ever. Microsoft has found, for example, that when managers help

Idea in Brief

The Problem

Managers are the lifeblood of organizations. In recent decades, as the workplace has changed, they've been asked to take on new responsibilities and demonstrate new skills—and are struggling to cope. This threatens productivity, employee well-being, and brand reputation.

The New Reality

Change has come along three dimensions: power (managers have to think about making teams successful, not being served by them); skills (they're expected to coach performance, not oversee tasks); and structure (they have to lead in more fluid environments).

The Way Forward

We need to do everything we can to help managers adapt. The three companies featured in this article have deliberately—and successfully—transformed the role of manager so that it better meets the demands of 21st-century work.

teams prioritize, nurture their culture, and support work/life balance, employees feel more connected and are more positive about their work. The consulting firm O.C. Tanner has likewise found that weekly one-to-ones with managers during uncertain times lead to a 54% increase in engagement, a 31% increase in productivity, a 15% decrease in burnout, and a 16% decrease in depression among employees. Meanwhile, according to McKinsey, having good relationships with their managers is the top factor in employees' job satisfaction, which in turn is the second-most-important determinant of their overall well-being.

Conversely, bad managers can significantly hurt retention and engagement: Seventy-five percent of the participants in the McKinsey survey reported that the most stressful aspect of their jobs was their immediate boss. As the saying goes, people join companies and leave their managers.

Something is clearly broken. If managers remain essential but their traditional role has become obsolete, then it's obviously time for a change.

In this article we'll make the case for redefining and even splitting the role rather than simply continuing to let it evolve, which is a potentially costly and disastrous course of action. But first let's briefly take stock of the waves of innovation that have brought us to this crisis point.

Four Defining Business Movements

The first wave, *process reengineering,* began about 1990 and lasted until the early 2000s. It focused on eliminating bureaucracy and boosting operational efficiencies. With the help of consulting firms, which developed practices around this kind of work, companies globalized and outsourced their processes, flattened their hierarchies, and in many cases put their remaining managers in "player-coach" roles that required them to take on workers' tasks. These changes reduced costs, but they also made life a lot harder for managers. They now had wider responsibilities and significantly larger teams to supervise and were also expected to dedicate themselves personally to projects and customers.

The next wave of innovation, *digitization,* arrived in about 2010. Promisingly, it democratized access to both information and people, but in doing so it undermined traditional sources of managerial power. CEOs and other senior leaders could now communicate directly with their entire workforces, sharing strategies, priorities, and important updates and responding to concerns. No longer a necessary part of the information loop, managers began to feel a loss of power, control, and status.

Then came the *agile movement* and its process changes, which companies began to adopt in the mid to late 2010s. It aimed to shorten timelines and turbocharge innovation by using internal marketplaces across whole organizations to match skills to work and to rapidly assemble project teams on an as-needed basis. As a result, managers started to lose touch with their reports, who now spent much of their time under the rotating supervision of the project managers they were temporarily assigned to. And because candidates could be matched to openings online, managers lost the power and authority involved with brokering career opportunities for their people.

Finally, a fourth wave arrived in 2020 with the pandemic, when companies and employees were forced to embrace the possibilities of *flexible work*. This was a watershed moment. It dramatically altered how and where work was done. Once employees were no longer tied to a physical workplace, managers lost the close control that they used to have over employees' performance and behavior—and employees began to realize that they could tap a greater range of job options, far beyond commuting distance from their homes. These changes were liberating, but they placed even more of a burden on managers—who now were also expected to cultivate empathetic relationships that would allow them to engage and retain the people they supervised.

These waves of innovation have changed the role of the manager along three dimensions: *power, skills,* and *structure.* In a power shift, managers have to think about making teams successful, not being served by them. In a skills shift, they're expected to coach performance, not oversee tasks; and in a structural shift, they have to lead in more fluid environments. (See the exhibit "From manager to people leader.")

These changes have empowered employees, which of course is a good thing. But they've also altered how managers drive productivity. Organizations are starting to recognize this. When we asked the executives in our 60-company survey to list the most important areas that managers need to focus on today, their top answers were coaching, communication, and employee well-being.

New Models of Management

Some organizations have taken deliberate steps to reimagine the role of the manager. Let's take a look at transformative shifts that have been made at three very different companies in banking, tech, and telecommunications.

Building new skills at scale

Most companies think of their top leaders as the people who make change happen—and are willing to spend millions on their

From manager to people leader

Three fundamental shifts in the role of managers today

A power shift: from "me" to "we"

My team makes me successful.	⟶ I'm here to make my team successful.
I'm rewarded for achieving business goals.	⟶ I'm also rewarded for improving team engagement, inclusion, and skills relevancy.
I control how people move beyond my unit.	⟶ I scout for talent and help my team move fluidly to wider opportunities.

A skills shift: from task overseer to performance coach

I oversee work.	⟶ I track outcomes.
I assess team members against expectations.	⟶ I coach them to achieve their potential and invite their feedback on my management.
I provide work direction and share information from above.	⟶ I supply inspiration, sensemaking, and emotional support.

A structural shift: from static and physical to fluid and digital

I manage an intact team of people in fixed jobs in a physical workplace.	⟶ My team is fluid, and the workplace is digital.
I set goals and make assessments annually.	⟶ I provide ongoing guidance on priorities and performance feedback.
I hold an annual career discussion focused on the next promotion.	⟶ I'm always retraining my team and providing career coaching.

development as a result. The layers of management below the top, the theory goes, are frozen in place and will resist change. But the executives at Standard Chartered—a retail bank, headquartered in London, with more than 750 branches in 50-plus countries—recently chose to think differently. Their 14,000 middle managers, they decided, would play a central role in the bank's growth.

Rather than wholly redesigning the job, the executive team began with some basic steps: changing the role's title, creating an accreditation process, and strengthening the sense of a managerial community. Managers became "people leaders," an acknowledgment of how important the human connection was in their work. Meanwhile, the new accreditation process evaluated future-focused capabilities such as driving growth, building trust, aligning teams, and making bold decisions. And the executive team worked to strengthen community by applying the local experiences of people leaders to problems across the whole company. For example, when in the course of filling 10 positions, one cohort of people leaders failed to hire anybody from an underrepresented group, the executive team didn't single the group out for criticism but instead seized the opportunity to ask the whole community, "How can we support you in making your teams more diverse?"

Next the executive team decided to focus on coaching, which has today become a crucial management skill. (See "The Leader as Coach," by Herminia Ibarra and Anne Scoular, HBR, November–December 2019.) Coaching, in fact, plays a key role in each of the three shifts we described earlier: When managers coach they're making a power shift by moving from instruction to support and guidance; a skills shift by moving from the oversight of work to the continual giving of feedback; and a structural shift by engaging with their people in a way that's dynamic and constant rather than static and episodic.

Standard Chartered had been working for decades on developing its top leaders into coaches. But now the challenge was scaling that effort up to 14,000 people leaders. The bank did this through a variety of initiatives—by using an AI-based coaching platform, for example, and by developing peer-to-peer and team coaching across all its markets in Africa, the Middle East, and Asia. It also launched a pilot project in which it offered to help people leaders pay for formal training and accreditation as coaches (by outside organizations approved by the global governing body for coaching). Those who accepted were expected to coach other employees; the goal was building what Tanuj Kapilashrami, the bank's

Three Questions About Hybrid Performance Management, Answered

by Tsedal Neeley

EXTENSIVE DATA ACROSS SURVEYS INDICATES THAT MOST people want hybrid work arrangements—that is, a mix of in-person and remote work—as we continue to move through the pandemic. For example, Microsoft's 2021 Work Trend Index, a study of more than 30,000 people in 31 countries, found that 73% of respondents desire remote work options. FlexJobs surveyed more than 2,100 people who worked remotely during the pandemic and found that 58% would leave their jobs if they weren't able to continue working from home at least some of the time.[a]

Recently I called on readers to send me their questions about transitioning to hybrid work. I've answered three of the most frequently asked ones here.

1. How do we ensure that proximity bias doesn't affect career advancement?

For hybrid work to actually work, managers must understand that out of sight doesn't mean out of mind. Remote members of a hybrid team will often wonder whether they fare differently than colocated workers who can catch the boss's ear in person. For example, they may worry they will be evaluated more harshly or given lower performance reviews than their in-office peers. It's incumbent upon managers to ensure that these fears are not realized.

Providing adequate feedback, and developing and promoting people without proximity bias, is crucial. Working remotely won't have a negative impact on relationships or the task dimensions of job performance as long as managers' evaluations of remote workers are as fair as those of colocated ones.

2. How do we measure the performance of remote or hybrid employees?

The great remote-work experiment disrupted companies' reliance on butts-in-seats presenteeism to measure performance. When managers aren't in the same space as their teams most of the time, they must instead measure performance based on outcomes, group cohesion, and individual development.[b]

First, assess whether people are *delivering results*—in other words, achieving expected goals. Second, ensure the team is *operating as one cohesive unit*. Learning how to work together as a group, rather than as individuals in silos, is what creates a successful hybrid team. Finally, support *individual growth* as a function of being on the team. When team members have the space to grow, expand their knowledge, acquire new skills, and learn new perspectives, their job satisfaction increases and they become more capable.

Once goals in all three areas are clearly in place, managers should empower, equip, coach, and assess performance according to outcomes instead of micromanaging every single task.

3. How can we foster trust among teammates who seldom see one another in person?

Just like groups, trust comes in many shapes and sizes. In-person teams start from our more natural mindset of being cautiously skeptical and building trust over time, but hybrid or remote groups need to flip the script: Start from a mindset of having confident trust in one another, and work from there. Sure, challenges could arise that shake our trust, in which case we need to adjust our expectations. But it's much more likely that people will prove us right, because trust inspires trust. It's a virtuous cycle.

Two types of trust have proven to be most effective in groups of people who don't share the same space routinely: *cognitive swift trust* and *emotional trust*. Cognitive swift trust is the willingness of team members to depend on one another based on sufficient evidence of reliability and competence. While swift trust isn't as complete as what's built when people are able to get to know one another over time, it's sufficient for completing shared tasks effectively.

By comparison, emotional trust is grounded in the belief that coworkers and managers have care and concern for us. When that kind of trust is present, people feel connection, a sense of closeness. As Theodore Roosevelt famously said, "People don't care how much you know until they know how much you care." Empathetic words, actions, and self-disclosures that occur in meetings, emails, chats, or online posts can nurture emotional trust.

Managers of hybrid groups can also feed trust with activities during "structured unstructured time" that make members more familiar with one another's personalities and values. These exchanges may occur more informally when everyone is collocated, but they can still be facilitated through virtual lunches, happy hours, coffee chats, or online games.

a. Rachel Pelta, "FlexJobs Survey Finds Employees Want Remote Work Post-Pandemic," n.d., FlexJobs, https://www.flexjobs.com/blog/post/flexjobs-survey-finds-employees-want-remote-work-post-pandemic/.
b. J. Richard Hackman, *Leading Teams: Setting the Stage for Great Performances* (Boston: Harvard Business Review Press, 2002).

Adapted from "12 Questions About Hybrid Work, Answered," on hbr.org, September 28, 2021 (product #H06LGU).

head of human resources, describes as "a deep coaching culture." So many participants reported a boost in skills and confidence that the bank organized further rounds of training and accreditation, each of which was oversubscribed, with hundreds of people taking part around the world.

Rewiring processes and systems

In 2013, as IBM's new chief human resources officer, Diane realized that to support the massive transformation that had been launched by then-CEO Ginni Rometty, the company needed a different kind of manager. IBM was changing 50% of its product portfolio over the next five years, moving into several growth businesses (among them the cloud, AI, cybersecurity, and blockchain), and migrating from software licensing to software as a service. At a worldwide town hall, Rometty announced that all employees would be required not only to develop new skills but also to learn to work differently. The company would build a culture optimized for innovation and speed—and needed its managers to lead retraining efforts, adapt their management styles to agile work methods, and get all employees engaged in the journey.

That meant doing three things: freeing managers up for additional responsibilities by digitally transforming their work; equipping them with new skills; and holding them accountable through a metrics-driven performance-development system. Their most important goal was employee engagement: Managers account for 70% of the variance in that metric.

The HR function deployed AI to eliminate administrative work, such as approving expense reports or transferring employees to a new unit. Personalized digital learning was introduced so that managers could access support on their mobile phones—for, say, just-in-time guidance on preparing for difficult conversations. New AI-driven programs also helped managers make better people decisions and spot issues like attrition risk. An AI-driven adviser has made it easier for managers to determine salary increases: It considers not only performance and market pay gaps but also internal data on employee turnover by skills, the current external demand for each employee's skills (scraped from competitor job postings), and the future demand.

Now when managers have salary conversations with employees, they can confidently share the rationale for their decisions, help team members understand the demand for their skills, and, most important, focus on supporting them as they build market-relevant capabilities and accelerate their career growth.

Like Standard Chartered, IBM also introduced an accreditation for managers, built on a new training curriculum. The impact has been significant: Managers who have obtained this accreditation are scoring five points higher today on employee engagement than those who have not.

In addition, IBM requires managers to get "licenses" in key activities by undergoing an in-house certification program. Licenses to hire, for example, are designed to ensure that managers select candidates in an objective and unbiased way, provide them with a well-designed experience, and ultimately make hires of high quality. The impact has been significant here too: Employees hired by licensed managers are 7% more likely to exceed expectations at six months and 45% less likely to leave the company within their first year than other hires are. Those numbers mean a lot in a company that makes more than 50,000 hires a year.

One major shift is the deliberate change from performance management to performance development. Not just about business results, the new system reflects the mindset and skills needed to manage in the modern workplace.

Feedback is at its core. Team members are asked whether their managers create an environment that encourages candid communication. Do they provide frequent and meaningful feedback? Do they help in the development of market-relevant skills? Are they effective career coaches? At the same time, HR gathers metrics on diversity and inclusion, regretted attrition, and skills development. The company then combines those metrics with its survey data and feeds the results into its Manager Success Index—a dashboard that allows managers to understand how well they're meeting expectations and to identify needs for both learning and "unlearning." Managers are invited to training programs on the basis of their specific development needs. Investing in these programs pays off: People who have completed at least one course in the past two years are 20% less likely to be in the bottom decile of the Manager Success Index, whereas those who have taken no leadership development courses are much more likely to be there.

IBM takes this idea seriously. Managers who do not demonstrate growth behaviors and who consistently underperform get moved out of managerial positions. The message to the company's managers is clear: Times have changed, and you must too. Your ongoing service as a manager is tightly connected to the continued growth and engagement of your people. We're here to support you in rethinking traditional practices, attitudes, and habits, and adopting ones better suited to new ways of working and the digital workplace.

Splitting the role of the manager

Telstra, a $16 billion Australian telecommunications company that employs more than 32,000 people, has made perhaps the boldest move. When Telstra's CEO, Andy Penn, decided to make the company more customer-focused, fast-paced, and agile, he and his chief human resources officer, Alex Badenoch, dramatically flattened its hierarchy, reducing the number of organizational layers to three.

Penn, Badenoch, and their team recognized that the restructuring provided a perfect opportunity to redesign the managerial job. "This change has been needed for so long," Badenoch told us. "We realized we had to separate work and management and create two distinct roles: *leader of people* and *leader of work.*" With very few exceptions, this new model applies to the entire organization.

Leaders of people are responsible for similarly skilled employees grouped into guildlike "chapters"—one for financial planners, say, and another for people experienced in change implementation. Most chapters consist of several hundred people, but some are larger. Subchapter leaders one level below are responsible for 15 to 20 members with narrower specializations and are located all over the world. What people do—not where they are—is what matters most.

Leaders of people ensure that the employees in their chapters have the skills and capabilities to meet the current and future needs of the business. They also help chapter members develop pathways to other chapters, to broaden insights and avoid silos. "The role of leaders of people," Badenoch told us, "is to know people beyond their work, to understand their career aspirations, to feed their minds and create thought provocations." Their performance is judged by such standards as how engaged they are with the people on their teams (measured by net promoter scores) and how well they fulfill requirements, among them the amount of time that their people are actively at work on projects, as opposed to being "on the bench."

Leaders of work focus on the flow of work and the commercial imperatives of the business. They don't directly manage people or control operating budgets. Instead, they create and execute work plans and determine which chapters to draw from for them. These leaders' performance is judged by such standards as the clarity of their planning, the quality of their estimates, and whether their projects are on time and on budget. (See the sidebar "Telstra's Dual Manager Model.")

This bold experiment has been widely acclaimed internally. "You actually get two people out of it who are dedicated to your development," one employee commented. "Your chapter lead [leader of people] is there to talk to you about your growth, and you get to have some great, powerful conversations about the type of work you want to do and how to get there. You can be very honest and share your aspirations openly with them. They have an amazing network and can get you assignments that allow you to explore different roles. And your project leader [leader of work] is there on a day-to-day basis to provide you direction on the work you need to do and on the business outcomes that we're trying to deliver."

At Telstra neither group of leaders is subordinate to the other. Their pay ranges are the same, and they participate as equals in the senior leadership team. Together they determine what Badenoch calls "the equation of work," which reveals "who is performing well, and what the skill and capacity is." Leaders of people have a sense of

Telstra's Dual Manager Model

TO BETTER COPE with what it calls the new "equation of work," the telecommunications firm Telstra has flattened its hierarchy and split the traditional role of manager into two jobs: one devoted to people and the other to process. The two types of managers are equals and coordinate closely with each other.

Leader of people	Leader of work
Leads a global chapter of employees with similar skills	Leads an agile project team drawn from chapters and external contractors
Owns the talent capacity, including personnel budgets	Owns the work, including project plans and budgets
Forecasts skills gaps and closes them through training and hiring	Forecasts demand for skills
Selects employees for projects	Bids for employees
Is responsible for employee engagement, career movement, and skills	Is responsible for project deliverables and business outcomes

the dynamics of their talent pool, and leaders of work have a sense of the dynamics of workflow. By coordinating with their counterparts, leaders of people can anticipate skills gaps and prioritize training investments, or forecast undercapacity and the need for hiring—all while being mindful of the commitments, health, and well-being of employees.

This bifurcated model of management isn't new. It's been used for years in consulting, where one often finds a division between practice leadership and project leadership. What is new here is the context. Telstra has proven that the model can work effectively and profitably across all functions in big companies that have adopted agile practices and flexible work arrangements.

Let's step back and consider where we are. For roughly a century our approach to management was conventionally hierarchical. That made sense because work was organized sequentially and in silos, jobs were fixed, workspaces were physical, and information flowed downward. But that's no longer the case. In today's world of work, enabled by digitization, we prioritize agility, innovation, responsiveness, speed, and the value of human connection. All of that demands the new approach to management that we've discussed: one that involves shifts in power, skills, and structure.

We have to get this right. At no time in the past has the investor community paid such close attention to human capital in corporations—checking Glassdoor for signals of toxic work environments, demanding disclosure of metrics such as diversity and employee turnover. As the stewards of culture, managers are the lifeblood of organizations. The current state of overwhelmed, confused, and underskilled managers creates significant risk, not just to productivity and employee well-being but also to brand reputation.

Sometimes it takes a jolt like the new titles at Telstra and Standard Chartered, or the Manager Success Index at IBM, to signal that change is afoot. But in all cases the march to sustainable behavioral change is long. The Telstra experience shows us the benefits of a radical new organizational design, and the Standard Chartered and IBM experiences show us that at a minimum companies can take deliberate steps to shift managers' mindsets, energy, and focus. With these kinds of actions—which institutionalize change—we can ensure that people get the leadership they need in the new world of work.

Originally published in March–April 2022. Reprint R2202F

Creating Sustainable Performance

by Gretchen Spreitzer and Christine Porath

WHEN THE ECONOMY'S IN TERRIBLE SHAPE, when any of us is lucky to have a job—let alone one that's financially and intellectually rewarding—worrying about whether or not your employees are happy might seem a little over-the-top. But in our research into what makes for a consistently high-performing workforce, we've found good reason to care: Happy employees produce more than unhappy ones over the long term. They routinely show up at work, they're less likely to quit, they go above and beyond the call of duty, and they attract people who are just as committed to the job. Moreover, they're not sprinters; they're more like marathon runners, in it for the long haul.

So what does it mean to be happy in your job? It's not about *contentment*, which connotes a degree of complacency. When we and our research partners at the Ross School of Business's Center for Positive Organizational Scholarship started looking into the factors involved in sustainable individual and organizational performance, we found a better word: *thriving*. We think of a thriving workforce as one in which employees are not just satisfied and productive but also engaged in creating the future—the company's and their own. Thriving employees have a bit of an edge—they are highly energized—but they know how to avoid burnout.

Across industries and job types, we found that people who fit our description of thriving demonstrated 16% better overall performance (as reported by their managers) and 125% less burnout (self-reported) than their peers. They were 32% more committed to the organization and 46% more satisfied with their jobs. They also missed much less work and reported significantly fewer doctor visits, which meant health care savings and less lost time for the company.

We've identified two components of thriving. The first is *vitality*: the sense of being alive, passionate, and excited. Employees who experience vitality spark energy in themselves and others. Companies generate vitality by giving people the sense that what they do on a daily basis makes a difference.

The second component is *learning*: the growth that comes from gaining new knowledge and skills. Learning can bestow a technical advantage and status as an expert. Learning can also set in motion a virtuous cycle: People who are developing their abilities are likely to believe in their potential for further growth.

The two qualities work in concert; one without the other is unlikely to be sustainable and may even damage performance. Learning, for instance, creates momentum for a time, but without passion it can lead to burnout. What will I do with what I've learned? Why should I stick with this job? Vitality alone—even when you love the kudos you get for delivering results—can be deadening: When the work doesn't give you opportunities to learn, it's just the same thing over and over again.

The combination of vitality and learning leads to employees who deliver results and find ways to grow. Their work is rewarding not just because they successfully perform what's expected of them today but also because they have a sense of where they and the company are headed. In short, they are thriving, and the energy they create is contagious.

How Organizations Can Help Employees Thrive

Some employees thrive no matter the context. They naturally build vitality and learning into their jobs, and they inspire the people around them. A smart hiring manager will look for those people. But

Idea in Brief

Research has shown that managers can take four measures to help employees thrive at work. All four are necessary to promote a culture of vitality and learning.

Provide Decision-Making Discretion

Facebook employees are encouraged to "move fast and break things"—they have lots of leeway to solve problems on their own.

Share Information

Workers at Zingerman's restaurants—right down to the busboys—get up-to-the-minute feedback on every aspect of the

business, from customer satisfaction ratings to the number of dirty mugs in the sink.

Minimize Incivility

Leaders at Caiman Consulting attribute the firm's 95% retention rate to a culture in which background checks look for a reputation for civility.

Offer Performance Feedback

The mortgage finance company Quicken Loans has dashboards showing continually updated data on individual and team performance against goals.

most employees are influenced by their environment. Even those predisposed to flourish can fold under pressure.

The good news is that—without heroic measures or major financial investments—leaders and managers can jump-start a culture that encourages employees to thrive. That is, managers can overcome organizational inertia to promote thriving and the productivity that follows it—in many cases with a relatively modest shift in attention.

Ideally, you'd be blessed with a workforce full of people who naturally thrive. But there's a lot you can do to release and sustain enthusiasm. Our research has uncovered four mechanisms that create the conditions for thriving employees: providing decision-making discretion, sharing information, minimizing incivility, and offering performance feedback. The mechanisms overlap somewhat. For instance, if you let people make decisions but give them incomplete information, or leave them exposed to hostile reactions, they'll suffer rather than thrive. One mechanism by itself will get you part of the way, but all four are necessary to create a culture of thriving. Let's look at each in turn.

Providing Decision-Making Discretion

Employees at every level are energized by the ability to make decisions that affect their work. Empowering them in this way gives them a greater sense of control, more say in how things get done, and more opportunities for learning.

The airline industry might seem like an unlikely place to find decision-making discretion (let alone a thriving workforce), but consider one company we studied, Alaska Airlines, which created a culture of empowerment that has contributed to a major turnaround over the past decade. In the early 2000s the airline's numbers were flagging, so senior management launched the 2010 Plan, which explicitly invited employee input into decisions that would improve service while maintaining a reputation for timely departures. Employees were asked to set aside their current perceptions of "good" service and consider new ways to contribute, coming up with ideas that could take service from good to truly great.

Agents embraced the program, which gave them, for instance, the discretion to find solutions for customers who had missed flights or were left behind for any other reason. Ron Calvin, the director of the eastern region, told us of a call he had recently received on his cell phone from a customer he hadn't seen or spoken to since working at the Seattle airport, five years earlier. The customer had a three-month-old grandchild who had just gone into cardiac arrest. The grandparents were trying to get back to Seattle from Honolulu. Everything was booked. Ron made a few calls and got them on a flight right away. That day the grandfather sent Ron a text saying, simply, "We made it."

Efforts like this to meet individual needs without holding up flights have led to a number one rating for on-time performance and a full trophy case. The airline has also expanded considerably into new markets, including Hawaii, the Midwest, and the East Coast.

Southwest is a better-known story, largely because of the company's reputation for having a fun and caring culture. Flight attendants are often eager to sing, joke around, and in general entertain customers. They also radiate energy and a passion for learning. One

About the Research

OVER THE PAST SEVEN YEARS, we have been researching the nature of thriving in the workplace and the factors that enhance or inhibit it.

Across several studies with our colleagues Cristina Gibson and Flannery Garnett, we surveyed or interviewed more than 1,200 white- and blue-collar employees in an array of industries, including higher education, health care, financial services, maritime, energy, and manufacturing. We also studied metrics reflecting energy, learning, and growth, based on information supplied by employees and bosses, along with retention rates, health, overall job performance, and organizational citizenship behaviors.

We developed a definition of thriving that breaks the concept into two factors: *vitality*—the sense that you're energized and alive; and *learning*—the gaining of knowledge and skills. When you put the two together, the statistics are striking. For example, people who were high energy and high learning were 21% more effective as leaders than those who were only high energy. The outcomes on one measure in particular—health—were even more extreme. Those who were high energy and low learning were 54% worse when it came to health than those who were high in both.

decided to offer the preflight safety instructions in rap format. He was motivated to put his special talents to work, and the passengers loved it, reporting that it was the first time they had actually paid attention to the instructions.

At Facebook, decision-making discretion is fundamental to the culture. One employee posted a note on the site expressing his surprise, and pleasure, at the company's motto, "Move fast and break things," which encourages employees to make decisions and act. On just his second day of work, he found a fix to a complicated bug. He expected some sort of hierarchical review, but his boss, the vice president of product, just smiled and said, "Ship it." He marveled that so early on he had delivered a solution that would instantly reach millions of people.

The challenge for managers is to avoid cutting back on empowerment when people make mistakes. Those situations create the best conditions for learning—not only for the parties concerned but also for others, who can learn vicariously.

Sharing Information

Doing your job in an information vacuum is tedious and uninspiring; there's no reason to look for innovative solutions if you can't see the larger impact. People can contribute more effectively when they understand how their work fits with the organization's mission and strategy.

Alaska Airlines has chosen to invest management time in helping employees gain a broad view of the company's strategy. The 2010 Plan was launched with traditional communications but also with a months-long road show and training classes designed to help employees share ideas. The CEO, the president, and the COO still go on the road quarterly to gather information about the idiosyncrasies of various markets; they then disseminate what they've learned. The benefits show up in yearly measures of employee pride in the company—now knocking it out of the park at 90%.

At Zingerman's (an Ann Arbor, Michigan, community of food-related businesses that has worked closely with Wayne Baker, a colleague of ours in the Center for Positive Organizational Scholarship), information is as transparent as possible. The organization had never consciously withheld its numbers—financial information was tacked up for employees to see—but when cofounders Ari Weinzweig and Paul Saginaw studied open book management in the mid-1990s, they came to believe that employees would show more interest if they got involved in the "game."

Implementation of a more formal and meaningful open book policy was not easy. People could look at the numbers, but they had little reason to pay attention and didn't get much insight into how the data related to their daily work. For the first five or six years, the company struggled to build the concept into its systems and routines and to wrap people's minds around what Baker calls "the rigor of the huddle": weekly gatherings around a whiteboard at which teams track results, "keep score," and forecast the next week's numbers. Although people understood the rules of open book management, at first they didn't see the point of adding yet another meeting to their busy schedules. It wasn't until senior

By the Numbers

- Blue-collar workers who scored high on thriving performed 27% better overall than their lower-thriving colleagues.

- Thriving blue-collar workers were 53% more likely to experience positive career progression than other employees.

- White-collar workers who scored high on thriving performed 16% better overall than peers with lower scores.

leaders made huddling nonnegotiable that employees grasped the true purpose of the whiteboards, which displayed not just financial figures but also service and food quality measures, check averages, internal satisfaction figures, and "fun," which could mean anything from weekly contests to customer satisfaction ratings to employees' ideas for innovation.

Some Zingerman's businesses began instituting "mini games": short-term incentives to fix a problem or capitalize on an opportunity. For instance, the staff at Zingerman's Roadhouse restaurant used the greeter game to track how long it took for customers to be greeted. "Ungreeted" customers expressed less satisfaction, and employees found themselves frequently comping purchases to make up for service lapses. The greeter game challenged the host team to greet every customer within five minutes of being seated, with a modest financial reward for 50 straight days of success. It inspired hosts to quickly uncover and fix holes in the service process. Service scores improved considerably over the course of a month. Other Zingerman's businesses started similar games, with incentives for faster delivery, fewer knife injuries in the bakery (which would lower insurance costs), and neater kitchens.

The games have naturally created some internal tensions by delivering bad news along with the good, which can be demoralizing. But overall they have greatly increased frontline employees' sense of ownership, contributing to better performance. From 2000 to 2010 Zingerman's revenue grew by almost 300%, to more than $35 million; the company's leaders credit open book management as a key factor in that success.

Simple anecdotes lend credence to their claim. For instance, a couple of years ago we saw Ari Weinzweig give a talk at the Roadhouse. A guest asked him whether it was realistic to expect the average waiter or busboy to understand company strategy and finance. In response, Ari turned to a busboy, who had been oblivious to the conversation: Would the teenager mind sharing Zingerman's vision and indicating how well the restaurant was meeting its weekly goals? Without batting an eye, the busboy stated the vision in his own words and then described how well the restaurant was doing that week on "meals sent back to the kitchen."

While Zingerman's is a fairly small business, much larger ones—such as Whole Foods and the transportation company YRC Worldwide—have also adopted open book management. Systems that make information widely available build trust and give employees the knowledge they need to make good decisions and take initiative with confidence.

Minimizing Incivility

The costs of incivility are great. In our research with Christine Pearson, a professor at Thunderbird School of Global Management, we discovered that half of employees who had experienced uncivil behavior at work intentionally decreased their efforts. More than a third deliberately decreased the quality of their work. Two-thirds spent a lot of time avoiding the offender, and about the same number said their performance had declined.

Most people have experienced rude behavior at work. Here are a few quotes from our research:

"My boss asked me to prepare an analysis. This was my first project, and I was not given any instructions or examples. He told me the assignment was crap."

"My boss said, 'If I wanted to know what you thought, I'd ask you.'"

"My boss saw me remove a paper clip from some documents and drop it in my wastebasket. In front of my 12 subordinates he rebuked me for being wasteful and required me to retrieve it."

"On speakerphone, in front of peers, my boss told me that I'd done 'kindergarten work.'"

We have heard hundreds of stories, and they're sadly familiar to most working people. But we don't hear so much about the costs.

Incivility prevents people from thriving. Those who have been the targets of bad behavior are often, in turn, uncivil themselves: They sabotage their peers. They "forget" to copy colleagues on memos. They spread gossip to deflect attention. Faced with incivility, employees are likely to narrow their focus to avoid risks—and lose opportunities to learn in the process.

A management consultancy we studied, Caiman Consulting, was founded as an alternative to the larger firms. Headquartered in Redmond, Washington, in offices that are not particularly sleek, the firm is recognized for its civil culture. Background checks in its hiring process include a candidate's record of civility.

"People leave a trail," says Caiman's director, Greg Long. "You can save yourself from a corrosive culture by being careful and conscientious up front." The managing director, Raazi Imam, told us, "I have no tolerance for anyone to berate or disrespect someone." When it does happen, he pulls the offender aside to make his policy clear. Long attributes the firm's 95% retention rate to its culture.

Caiman passes up highly qualified candidates who don't match that culture. It also keeps a list of consultants who might be good hires when an appropriate spot opens up. The HR director, Meg Clara, puts strong interpersonal skills and emotional intelligence among her prime criteria for candidates.

At Caiman, as at all companies, managers establish the tone when it comes to civility. A single bad player can set the culture awry. One young manager told us about her boss, an executive who had a habit of yelling from his office, "You made a mistake!" for a sin as minor as a typo. His voice would resonate across the floor, making everyone cringe and the recipient feel acutely embarrassed. Afterward, colleagues would gather in a common area for coffee and commiseration. An insider told us that those conversations focused not on how to get ahead at the company or learn to cope by developing a thick skin but on how to get even and get out.

Individual Strategies for Thriving

ALTHOUGH ORGANIZATIONS BENEFIT from enabling employees to thrive, leaders have so much on their plates that attention to this important task can slip. However, anyone can adopt strategies to enhance learning and vitality without significant organizational support. And because thriving can be contagious, you may find your ideas quickly spreading.

Take a Break

Research by Jim Loehr and Tony Schwartz has shown that breaks and other renewal tactics, no matter how small, can create positive energy.

In our teaching, we let students design regular breaks and activities into the class to ensure that they stay energized. In one term, students decided to halt every class for two minutes at the midpoint to get up and do something active. Each week a different foursome designed the quick activity—watching a funny Youtube video, doing the cha-cha slide, or playing a game. The point is that the students figure out what is energizing for them and share it with the class.

Even if your organization doesn't offer formal mechanisms for renewal, it's nearly always possible to schedule a short walk, a bike ride, or a quick lunch in the park. Some people write it into their schedules so that meetings can't impinge.

Craft Your Own Work to Be More Meaningful

You can't ignore the requirements of your job, but you can watch for opportunities to make it more meaningful. Consider Tina, the staff administrator of a policy think tank within a large organization. When her boss took a six-month sabbatical, Tina needed to find a short-term replacement project. After some scouting, she uncovered a budding initiative to develop staff members' ability to speak up with their ideas about the organization. The effort needed an innovative spirit to kick it off. The pay was lower, but the nature of the work energized Tina. When her boss returned, she renegotiated the terms of her think tank job to consume only 80% of her time, leaving the rest for the staff development project.

Look for Opportunities to Innovate and Learn

Breaking out of the status quo can trigger the learning so essential to thriving. When Roger became the head of a prestigious high school in the Midwest, he was brimming with innovative ideas. He quickly ascertained, however, that quite a few staff members were not open to new ways of doing things. He made sure to listen to their concerns and tried to bring them along, but he invested more of his efforts in the growth and learning of those who shared his passion for breakthrough ideas. Mentoring and encouraging them, Roger began to achieve small wins, and his initiatives gained some momentum. A few of the resisters ended up leaving the school, and others came around when they saw signs of positive change. By focusing on those bright spots rather than the points of resistance, Roger was able to launch an effort that is propelling the school toward a radically different future.

Invest in Relationships That Energize You

All of us have colleagues who may be brilliant but are difficult and corrosive to work with. Individuals who thrive look for opportunities to work closely with colleagues who generate energy and to minimize interaction with those who deplete it. In fact, when we built the research team to study thriving, we chose colleagues we enjoyed, who energized us, with whom we looked forward to spending time, and from whom we knew we could learn. At the Center for Positive Organizational Scholarship, we seek to build good relationships by starting every meeting with good news or expressions of gratitude.

Recognize That Thriving Can Spill Over Outside the Office

There's evidence that high levels of engagement at work will not lessen your ability to thrive in your personal life but instead can enhance it. When one of us (Gretchen) was dealing with her husband's difficult medical diagnosis, she found that her work, even though it was demanding, gave her the energy to thrive professionally and in her family life. Thriving is not a zero-sum game. People who feel energized at work often bring that energy to their lives beyond work. And people inspired by outside activities—volunteering, training for a race, taking a class—can bring their drive back to the office.

In our research, we were surprised by how few companies consider civility—or incivility—when evaluating candidates. Corporate culture is inherently contagious; employees assimilate to their environment. In other words, if you hire for civility, you're more likely to breed it into your culture.

Offering Performance Feedback

Feedback creates opportunities for learning and the energy so critical for a culture of thriving. By resolving feelings of uncertainty, feedback keeps people's work-related activities focused on personal and organizational goals. The quicker and more direct the feedback, the more useful it is.

The Zingerman's huddle, described earlier, is a tool for sharing near-real-time information about individual as well as business performance. Leaders outline daily ups and downs on the whiteboard, and employees are expected to "own" the numbers and come up with ideas for getting back on track when necessary. The huddles also include "code reds" and "code greens," which document customer complaints and compliments so that all employees can learn and grow on the basis of immediate and tangible feedback.

Quicken Loans, a mortgage finance company that measures and rewards employee performance like no other organization, offers continually updated performance feedback using two types of dashboard—a ticker and kanban reports. (*Kanban,* a Japanese word meaning "signal," is used frequently in operations.)

The ticker has several panels displaying group and individual metrics along with data feeds that show how likely an employee is to meet his or her daily goals. People are hardwired to respond to scores and goals, so the metrics help keep them energized through the day; essentially, they're competing against their own numbers.

The kanban dashboard allows managers to track people's performance so that they know when an employee or a team needs some coaching or other type of assistance. A version of the kanban chart is also displayed on monitors, with a rotating list of the top 15 salespeople for each metric. Employees are constantly in competition to make the boards, which are almost like a video game's ranking of high scorers.

Employees could feel overwhelmed or even oppressed by the constant nature of the feedback. Instead, the company's strong norms for civility and respect and for giving employees a say in how they accomplish their work create a context in which the feedback is energizing and promotes growth.

The global law firm O'Melveny & Myers lauds the use of 360-degree evaluations in helping workers thrive. The feedback is open-ended and summarized rather than shared verbatim, which has encouraged a 97% response rate. Carla Christofferson, the managing partner of the Los Angeles office, learned from her evaluation that people saw her behavior as not matching the firm's stated commitment to work-life balance—which was causing stress among employees. She started to spend more time away from the office and to limit weekend work to things she could do at home. She became a role model for balance, which went a long way toward eliminating the worry of employees who wanted a life outside of work.

The four mechanisms that help employees thrive don't require enormous efforts or investments. What they do require is leaders who are open to empowering employees and who set the tone. As we noted earlier, each mechanism provides a different angle necessary for thriving. You can't choose one or two from the menu; the mechanisms reinforce one another. For example, can people be comfortable making decisions if they don't have honest information about current numbers? Can they make effective decisions if they're worried about being ridiculed?

Creating the conditions for thriving requires your concerted attention. Helping people grow and remain energized at work is valiant on its own merits—but it can also boost your company's performance in a sustainable way.

Originally published in January–February 2012. Reprint R1201F

JEAN-LOUIS BARSOUX is a term research professor at IMD. He is a coauthor of *ALIEN Thinking: The Unconventional Path to Breakthrough Ideas*.

MARCUS BUCKINGHAM is the head of people and performance research at the ADP Research Institute and a coauthor (with Ashley Goodall) of *Nine Lies About Work: A Freethinking Leader's Guide to the Real World* (Harvard Business Review Press, 2019). His most recent book is *Love + Work: How to Find What You Love, Love What You Do, and Do It for the Rest of Your Life* (Harvard Business Review Press, 2022).

TIMOTHY BUTLER is a senior fellow at Harvard Business School and senior adviser to its Career and Professional Development program. He is the author of *Getting Unstuck: A Guide to Discovering Your Next Career Path* (Harvard Business Review Press, 2010).

PETER CAPPELLI is the George W. Taylor Professor of Management at the Wharton School and a director of its Center for Human Resources. He is the author of several books, including *Will College Pay Off?: A Guide to the Most Important Financial Decision You'll Ever Make*.

HEIDI K. GARDNER is a distinguished fellow at Harvard Law School and a faculty chair in the school's executive education programs. She is also a cofounder of Gardner & Collaborators. Her most recent book is *Smarter Collaboration: How Professionals and Their Firms Succeed by Breaking Down Silos* (Harvard Business Review Press, 2022).

DIANE GHERSON is the former chief human resources officer of IBM and a senior lecturer of business administration at Harvard Business School.

ASHLEY GOODALL is the senior vice president of leadership and team intelligence at Cisco Systems and a coauthor (with Marcus Buckingham) of *Nine Lies About Work: A Freethinking Leader's Guide to the Real World* (Harvard Business Review Press, 2019).

LYNDA GRATTON is a professor of management practice at London Business School and the founder of HSM, the future-of-work research consultancy. Her most recent book, coauthored with Andrew J. Scott, is *The New Long Life: A Framework for Flourishing in a Changing World*.

MICHAEL HARRIS is a doctoral student at the University of North Carolina's Kenan-Flagler Business School.

JEAN-FRANÇOIS MANZONI is Professor of Leadership and Organizational Development at IMD. His award-winning research on boss-subordinate relationships includes *The Set-Up-to-Fail Syndrome: Overcoming the Undertow of Expectations* (with Jean-Louis Barsoux, Harvard Business School Press, 2007).

IVAN MATVIAK is an executive vice president at Clearwater Analytics.

TSEDAL NEELEY is the Naylor Fitzhugh Professor of Business Administration and senior associate dean of faculty and research at Harvard Business School. She is a coauthor of the book *The Digital Mindset: What It Really Takes to Thrive in the Age of Data, Algorithms, and AI* and the author of the book *Remote Work Revolution: Succeeding from Anywhere* and the online HarvardX course Remote Work Revolution for Everyone. Follow her on Twitter @tsedal.

MAURY A. PEIPERL is a pro-vice-chancellor of Cranfield University, in England, and the director of its School of Management.

CHRISTINE PORATH is a professor of management at Georgetown University and the author of *Mastering Community: The Surprising Ways Coming Together Moves Us from Surviving to Thriving* and *Mastering Civility: A Manifesto for the Workplace*.

GRETCHEN SPREITZER is the Keith E. and Valerie J. Alessi Professor of Business Administration at the University of Michigan's Ross School of Business, where she is a core faculty member in the Center for

Positive Organizations. Her most recent work looks at positive deviance and how organizations enable employees to thrive.

ANNA TAVIS is a clinical associate professor of human capital management at New York University and the Perspectives editor at *People + Strategy,* a journal for HR executives.

BILL TAYLER is the Robert J. Smith Professor at Brigham Young University's Marriott School of Business.

BEN WABER is the president and cofounder of the workplace analytics company Humanyze and the author of *People Analytics: How Social Sensing Technology Will Transform Business and What It Tells Us About the Future of Work.* Follow him on Twitter @bwaber.

JAMES WALDROOP is a founding principal of Peregrine Partners, a consulting firm in Brookline, Massachusetts, that specializes in executive development and employee retention.

MAXINE WILLIAMS is Facebook's global chief diversity officer.

Index

performance reviews at, 2, 8, 10, 11, 14–15, 19
digitization, 140
discrimination, 15–16, 127–130, 133
    gender, 129–130
    in hiring, 127–130, 133
    laws against, 4–5
    racial, 127–130
    workplace, 127–128
disengagement, by employees, 57
diversity, 128, 132
    See also underrepresented groups
    cognitive, 135
    metrics on, 147, 151
dopamine, 94

earnings, 122
emotional trust, 145
empathy, 138
employee development, 4, 6–8
    focus on, 8–9
    role of managers in, 147
    separating from compensation discussion, 104
employee motivation, 4, 48, 56
employee performance
    appraisal of. *See* performance appraisals
    creating sustainable, 153–165
    as fixed, 5
    "how" vs. "what" in, 105
    impact of appraisals on, 7
    impact of expectations on, 55–56
    recognition of, 25, 105
    rewarding, 14–15, 105
    strengthening, 27–30
    transactional view of, 2–3
    views on, 2–3
employees
    See also poor performers
    creative rewards for, 105

decision-making discretion by, 155, 156–157
disengagement by, 57
engagement of, 99, 103, 139
in-groups/out-groups, 50, 54–55, 60
habit tracking of, 107–108
happiness of, 153
identifying poorly performing, 15
information sharing with, 155, 158–160
minimizing incivility for, 155, 160–161, 164
people analytics and, 107–116
personal accountability of, 99–101
remote, 144–145
thriving, 153–165
empowerment, of employees, 155–157
enterprise control (life interest), 80, 81, 82, 89
executive compensation, 5
expectations, of boss, 27, 47–51, 55–56

Facebook, 134–135, 157
fairness, 68, 133
FastWorks platform, 9
feedback
    aligning frequency of, with work milestones, 104–105
    apps, 16, 18
    constructive, 40, 42
    continuous, 7, 11, 16, 18, 164–165
    delayed, 11
    frequent, 8, 9, 10
    importance of, 6
    instant, 1
    for managers, 147–148
    negative, 37
    offering, 155, 164–165

Engage with HBR content the way you want, on any device.

With HBR's subscription plans, you can access world-renowned case studies from Harvard Business School and receive four **free eBooks**. Download and customize prebuilt **slide decks and graphics** from our **Data & Visuals** collection. With HBR's archive, top 50 best-selling articles, and five new articles every day, HBR is more than just a magazine.

Subscribe Today
HBR.org/success

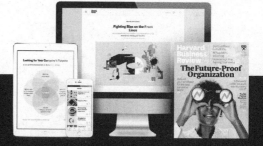

The most important management ideas all in one place.

We hope you enjoyed this book from *Harvard Business Review*. Now you can get even more with HBR's 10 Must Reads Boxed Set. From books on leadership and strategy to managing yourself and others, this 6-book collection delivers articles on the most essential business topics to help you succeed.

HBR's 10 Must Reads Series

The definitive collection of ideas and best practices on our most sought-after topics from the best minds in business.

- Change Management
- Collaboration
- Communication
- Emotional Intelligence
- Innovation
- Leadership
- Making Smart Decisions

- Managing Across Cultures
- Managing People
- Managing Yourself
- Strategic Marketing
- Strategy
- Teams
- The Essentials

hbr.org/mustreads

Engage with HBR content the way you want, on any device.

With HBR's subscription plans, you can access world-renowned case studies from Harvard Business School and receive four **free eBooks**. Download and customize prebuilt **slide decks and graphics** from our **Data & Visuals** collection. With HBR's archive, top 50 best-selling articles, and five new articles every day, HBR is more than just a magazine.

Subscribe Today
HBR.org/success

The most important management ideas all in one place.

We hope you enjoyed this book from *Harvard Business Review*. Now you can get even more with HBR's 10 Must Reads Boxed Set. From books on leadership and strategy to managing yourself and others, this 6-book collection delivers articles on the most essential business topics to help you succeed.

HBR's 10 Must Reads Series

The definitive collection of ideas and best practices on our most sought-after topics from the best minds in business.

- Change Management
- Collaboration
- Communication
- Emotional Intelligence
- Innovation
- Leadership
- Making Smart Decisions

- Managing Across Cultures
- Managing People
- Managing Yourself
- Strategic Marketing
- Strategy
- Teams
- The Essentials

hbr.org/mustreads